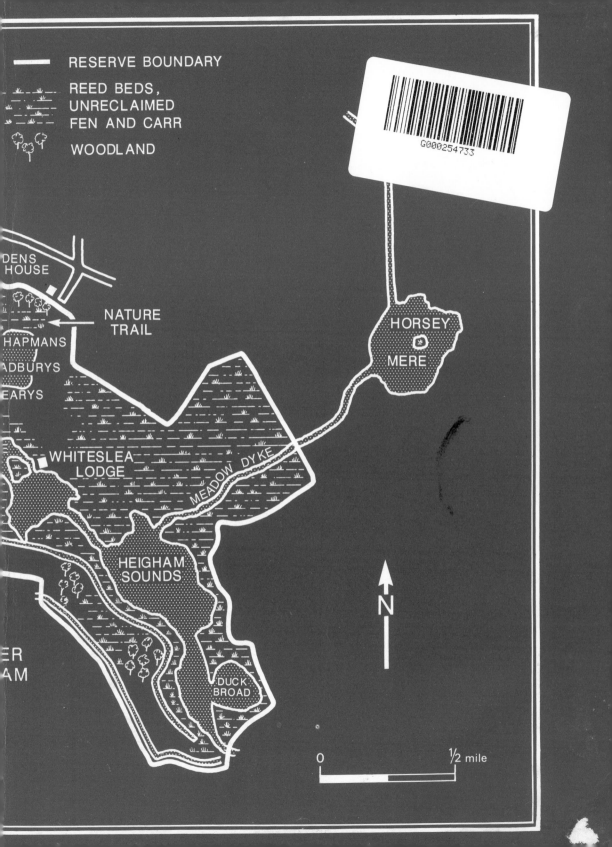

RESERVE BOUNDARY

REED BEDS,
UNRECLAIMED
FEN AND CARR

WOODLAND

DENS
HOUSE

NATURE
TRAIL

HAPMANS

ADBURYS

EARYS

WHITESLEA
LODGE

MEADOW DYKE

HORSEY
MERE

HEIGHAM
SOUNDS

DUCK
BROAD

ER

AM

N

0   ½ mile

HICKLING BROAD
AND ITS WILDLIFE

The Author and Norfolk's best-loved naturalist, Ted Ellis, about to go punting on Hickling Broad. February 1983.

Hickling Broad
and its Wildlife

The story of a famous wetland nature reserve

STEWART LINSELL

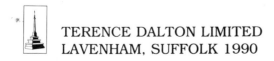

TERENCE DALTON LIMITED
LAVENHAM, SUFFOLK 1990

Published by
TERENCE DALTON LIMITED
ISBN 0 86138 072 X
© Stewart Linsell, 1990

TO KAY

It is a country of wide landscapes and magnificent sunsets, of high skies and awesome dawns, a land with a dignity of beauty peculiarly its own, of silences that are more potent than words.

J. Wentworth Day: *The Most English Corner of All England*

Text photoset in 10/11 pt Baskerville
Printed in Great Britain at
The Lavenham Press Limited, Lavenham, Suffolk

Contents

Foreword

By Christopher Cadbury, CBE, MA

HICKLING and Horsey have the only area of any size remaining as that relic of the once-vast areas of wetland extended over so much of East Anglia. As a result it has become internationally famous as a nature reserve, providing what is now a unique habitat for many rare species of British fauna and flora.

The Hickling shooting estate first gained its high reputation as a private nature reserve when it was managed for Lord Desborough by that outstanding ornithologist Jim Vincent, who was Lord

Hickling's great benefactor, Christopher Cadbury, at his home with Polo just before his eightieth birthday in 1988. S. Linsell

Desborough's head keeper from before the First World War until his death in 1944.

On the deaths of both Lord Desborough and Jim Vincent in 1944, the estate was acquired for the Norfolk Naturalists' Trust. In 1975 Stewart Linsell was appointed warden of Hickling; he is another talented ornithologist, well qualified to follow in the steps of the legendary Jim. He has the same enthusiasm and the same keen eyes and ears for identifying birds, including many rather obscure rarities. Perhaps even more important, like Jim Vincent he recognizes and understands the behaviour of the birds he is watching, knowing their peculiar movements and habits and also their requirements. This is a knowledge that comes only by long experience in the field.

With all these qualifications there could be no one more appropriate than Stewart Linsell to write about the history of the area and his fascinating experiences with wildlife. This book contains many personal anecdotes, which involve local people, and the reader is able to share in the delights and surprises of this special place, so ably described by the author.

Acknowledgements

THIS BOOK could not have been written without the kind and generous help of many friends. In particular, I thank Lord Buxton and Christopher Cadbury for reading the typescript and checking the historical background, and suggesting corrections; Ivor Vincent for permission to quote extracts from the diaries kept by his father from 1911 to 1944; Major J. D. Mills JP for information about his family's Hickling estate; and the Norfolk Naturalists' Trust for allowing me access to the deeds of the Whiteslea estate.

My thanks also to Gwen Amis, Arthur Beales, the late Ida Grosvenor, Billy Nudd, Colin Shingles and Betty Spooner for information, and anecdotes, about the past; James Cadbury for his botanical notes; Ivan Loades for his notes on dragonflies; Tim Peet for his essay on Lepidoptera; Michael Seago for casting a critical eye over the checklist of birds.

I am grateful to the following publishers and authors for permission to quote from these books: Country Life for the article by Lord William Percy on the bittern from *The Romance of Nature*; Country Life for extracts on the bittern and marsh and Montagu's harriers by Jim Vincent, also from *The Romance of Nature*; Country Life for extracts on the bearded tit and bittern from *Broadland Birds*, by Miss E. L. Turner; William Collins for the detailed account of the 1938 North Sea flood by Anthony Buxton from *Fisherman Naturalist*, and for the use of maps of Hickling Broad from *The Broads* by Ted Ellis; Dr Joyce Lambert for agreeing to my use of those maps; Batchworth Press Ltd for an account of the Hickling coot shoots from *At Dawn and Dusk*, by Colin McLean; Longman Group Ltd for extracts concerning visits to Hickling Broad by His Majesty King George VI from *The King in his Country*, by Aubrey (Lord) Buxton; Weidenfeld and Nicolson Ltd for extracts from *A Season of Birds*, by Edwin Vincent; Faber and Faber Ltd for an appreciation of Jim Vincent by George Yates from *Bird Haunts in Southern England*; Hutchinson and Co. Ltd for an appreciation of Jim Vincent by Eric Hosking from *An Eye for a Bird*; Greenrigg of Woodford Green for an extract from a poem by Stuart Boardman from *The Studio*; and the editor of *Shooting Times* for permission to use a Hickling fishing article by Denis Pye.

My thanks, too, to Gwen Amis, Marlene Belson, Margaret Bishop, John Buxton, Christopher Cadbury, Kevin Carlson, the *Eastern Daily Press*, Phyllis Ellis, the late Ida Grosvenor, Geoffrey

Hollis, Philip Judge, Jem Kime, Mike Linsell, Nigel Moore, Billy Nudd, the Norfolk Naturalists' Trust, Peter Steele Ivan West and Julia Turner for much illustrative material.

Finally, my special thanks to my long-suffering wife, Kay, who put up with the trials and tribulations of being married to a nature reserve warden; and to Teddy and Elizabeth Wall, who for so many years looked after our home and our dogs, kept my daily diary up to date, coped with the many visitors to the reserve, and enabled us to enjoy an annual holiday.

Members of the Hickling staff preparing the base for a new bird-hide, just a small part of the work that goes on to enable the public to see the local bird population in comfort. S. Linsell

Preface

ONE winter's day I was on the lookout at Whiteslea Lodge beside Hickling Broad. As I stood there and marvelled at the peaceful scene, ablaze with a riot of colour set off by the setting sun, I wondered about some of the people who had stood there in the past. What were the thoughts passing through the minds of King George V, King George VI or Prince Philip following a morning's wildfowling earlier this century? I looked down the long flight of steps and imagined I saw Lord Lucas, Lord Grey, Lord Desborough, Aubrey Buxton*, Hugh Wormald, and many other regular visitors coming up to see what the prospects were for the evening flight. Many a famous artist and photographer has also climbed those steps to the lookout and captured the superb views of the broad and marshes.

It dawned on me that Hickling Broad and its environs must have quite a story to tell. The second oldest nature reserve in the country, established privately in 1911, it must have a history to interest the naturalist; while tens of thousands of holidaymakers afloat on the broad over many decades must have gazed around them and wondered what had gone on there in the past as well as what happens today. Some odd things have occurred on the broad during my years as warden, and some of these I feel are worth relating.

The sun slowly sank blood-red below the horizon beyond Swim Coots. Water rails squealed in the reedbeds close by the lookout, and a couple of Cetti's warblers called; the vast horde of starlings which nightly roost in the more distant reedbeds now ceased to darken the sky as they settled down for the night; a barn owl flew past silently, heading towards the starlings and an easy meal; a great chorus came from the thousands of gulls which roost on the broad; and a flight of duck passed overhead on whistling wings as I descended the lookout steps.

Something prompted me to think about my modest library of natural history books. Did any of them have references to Hickling Broad? I checked book after book and was surprised and delighted to find that no fewer than twenty-eight did mention Hickling; best of all, I discovered I had copies of essays written over fifty years ago by such eminent naturalists as Lord William Percy, Jim Vincent and Emma Turner, all about Hickling's bird life.

Thus were the seeds of this book sown in my mind. This book is not written just for my fellow-naturalists; it has also been written

*now Lord Buxton of Alsa.

The changing face of Hickling: the south side of Duck Broad, where much of the fringe of reedswamp has vanished since the nineteen-seventies.   S. Linsell

for the holidaymaker who wishes to know something of the area, whether he sees it at the helm of a powerboat or a sailing cruiser or at the wheel of a car. Each year hundreds of holidaymakers arrive at Hickling, and are disappointed that all they can see of Hickling Broad is a view from the Pleasure Boat Inn staithe. This book describes better ways of seeing the broad. Scores of telephone calls are received from people wanting to know if the beautiful swallowtail butterfly, the bearded tit, the bittern, the marsh harrier, and other interesting species can be seen. These and others are referred to, some in considerable detail.

I am conscious of the fact that there are many aspects of the story of Hickling Broad and its wildlife to which I have not referred. In particular, some will note that there is no reference to the famous Hickling Broad court case of 1892; the story of this lengthy High Court action, still a matter of controversy in Hickling village, can be read in detail elsewhere. Anglers, too, may be disappointed that no mention has been made of the monster pike taken from waters once regarded as among the finest in Britain for coarse fishing; but at least we are reminded what fishing was like when the waters were still gin-clear, and the dreaded toxic alga *Prymnesium parvum* had not yet arrived.

I have in the space available endeavoured to tell something of the history of this unique wetland area, to cover some of the natural history disciplines, and to add some humour.

For information about visiting the reserve the intending visitor should write to the warden, Warden's House, Stubb Road, Hickling, Norwich NR12 0BW (telephone 069-261276).

A National Nature Reserve

HICKLING BROAD with Heigham Sounds, Horsey Mere and Martham Broad forms a unique ecological area with about 800 acres of open water, a last relic of the once-vast tracts of wet fen and marshland which were in the past such a feature of East Anglia. There was a time when it consisted of even larger areas of open water, meandering rivers, grazing marshes with graceful windmills and windpumps controlling water levels, and huge boggy marshes where in due season the reeds and sedges were harvested for thatchers, as they still are today. This is probably everyone's image of Broadland.

Perhaps some of the delegates at The Convention on Wetlands of International Importance at Ramsar in Iran in 1971 recalled visits to this wetland wilderness. They persuaded fellow delegates from most European countries to designate the area of Norfolk encompassed by Hickling, Potter Heigham, Martham, West Somerton, Horsey and Waxham one of the most important wetland areas in Europe, a designation which was ratified by the British Government five years later. The significance of that marvellous area of water and marsh, which had become Britain's second nature reserve as long ago as 1911, was thus internationally recognized. As a Ramsar site Hickling is afforded special protection through the Nature Conservancy Council, which as the Nature Conservancy had in 1957 declared the area a National Nature Reserve.

What is so special about this part of the Norfolk Broads? Those of us who have known this magical place over many decades find that its fauna and flora delight us; in spite of pollution in recent years there are some marsh dykes still rich in aquatic plants. The huge reedbeds and extensive areas of fen-type habitat retain much of their former wildness and beauty, thanks to past inundations by the North Sea and the presence of saltwater springs. The very openness of this part of the Broads is due to these saline conditions, which inhibit colonization by shrubs and trees. It is this open landscape beneath a vast umbrella of sky that is so very special.

As the sun finally sinks below the west end of Hickling Broad,

Opposite page: *The controlled flooding of grazing marshes in autumn proves a great attraction to wildfowl. By managing the land in this and other ways birds can be attracted to the reserve.* S. Linsell

turning its waters ruby-red, the holidaymaker afloat in his cruiser might be forgiven for thinking he is in Paradise.

This gem of a reserve holds many attractions for the wildlife enthusiast. The diversity of habitats has over the years attracted more than two hundred species of birds, including such Broadland specialities as the bearded tit, bittern, marsh harrier, Montagu's harrier, and Cetti's and Savi's warblers. Visitors come from all over Britain and from overseas to see our own indigenous swallowtail butterfly and its caterpillars. Fortunately an abundance of its host plant, milk parsley, thrives around the northern broads, which hold the greatest density of this spectacular butterfly. The mass displays of marsh flora, with meadowsweet, hemp agrimony, marsh valerian, purple and yellow loosestrife, angelica, marsh sowthistle, and many others, attract the botanists, while dragonfly specialists come hoping to see the rare Norfolk aeshna, *Aeshna isosceles.*

To appreciate the scenic beauty of this unique area and to see something of its wildlife, about which many authors have written down the ages, the visitor can participate in the very popular water trail, the first of its kind in Britain, founded in 1970, when it won a special Duke of Edinburgh Countryside Award. On this two-and-a-half-hour guided tour the 440-acre broad is crossed twice; visits are paid to hides overlooking wader pools where a fine variety of birds may be seen; a short walk through an area of fen on a hot summer's day produces swallowtail butterflies and many plant species; and the guide explains the harvests of reed and sedge. The highlight of the water trail for many, especially the young, is a visit to the sixty-foot-high tree tower in Whiteslea Wood. The view from this superb vantage point, which many will agree is the finest in Broadland, enables the visitor to appreciate to the full the open landscape of north-east Norfolk.

The walk through the wood to the tree tower is flanked by broad drifts of climbing corydalis, a plant which thrives in the peaty soil and enjoys the company of bracken. In spring and early summer chiffchaff, willow warbler, blackcap, turtle dove and many of our resident birds will be seen or heard, as will the drumming of both greater and lesser spotted woodpeckers. On a number of occasions golden orioles have been recorded on passage here. The tower itself has over the years given fine views of ospreys, red-footed falcon, hobby, red kite and sparrowhawk. Breeding marsh harriers may be seen quartering the marshes for prey for their young, but the chance of seeing a bittern is, sadly, very slim. Fine weather will bring pairs of swallowtails up through the oaks surrounding the tree tower, and in August purple hairstreak butterflies appear about the treetops.

For the visitors who climb the ladders to the tower mainly to enjoy the view there may be other rewards. A really wonderful sight is the silent and graceful passage of one of the restored Norfolk wherries or wherry yachts. It may be the *Albion*, built in 1898, with her enormous black sail, or the white-sailed wherry yachts *Olive* (1909) and *Norada* (1912). During the eighteenth and nineteenth centuries shallow-draught wherries were used commercially throughout Broadland carrying a variety of cargoes such as coal, timber, grain, bricks, and reed and marsh litter. They varied in size fom 25 to 40 tons, although the smallest was a mere five tons and the largest, significantly named *Wonder*, a full 80 tons[1]. On a really clear day ships can be seen out in the North Sea, and Horsey Mere, with its huge beds of reed and sedge and its grazing marshes, an extension of those at Hickling, can be seen as a thin pencil of water.

Whenever I was on the tree tower with visitors I made them look away to the far end of the broad, and then slowly northwards and eastwards to the distant coast, and impressed on them that this wonderful and unique area is safeguarded in perpetuity by the Norfolk Naturalists' Trust, the National Trust and the Nature Conservancy Council.

Broadland has a variety of moods that are enjoyed by many people in their own way. To old and young alike there is a time of

Duck Broad, a piece of water off Heigham Sounds greatly favoured by wildfowl. S. Linsell

day that has not changed over the centuries: be it spring or autumn, summer or winter, dawn is frequently magical.

This is the hour when mysterious shadows vanish before the rising sun. It would seem that this is one thing at least that has not changed much over many decades on Hickling. I have had the joyful experience on numerous occasions of witnessing the coming of dawn while seated on the lookout at Whiteslea Lodge, and of tape-recording every sound and movement of the awakening day. Dawn is the hour that belongs to Nature, and to those who are willing to rise and witness its splendour at the birth of a day when the skies are clear and the wind is but a murmur.

During spring and summer there is very little darkness in this land of windswept spaces, wide horizons, and vast silences. In such areas dawn can be very cold; vitality is at its lowest, and emotion, which stirs imagination, leaves one still colder. There are faint movements all around as creatures that move by night creep silently home to rest, while newly-awakened animals and birds stretch, yawn, and utter the first sounds of the day. The unexpected may happen, and the thought of it cheers one up.

The silence that so often ushers in a new day, especially in Broadland, is something tangible, almost audible. On windswept Hickling, tempestuous winds are frequently lulled an hour before sunrise, as if the very elements were awed at this daily miracle.

If you are on holiday on a boat, there is no especial merit attached to early rising; you wake up, and there you are—it is almost as good as being out of doors. During the breeding season some marsh birds seem to talk all night. Coots are great frequenters of night clubs. They chatter and squabble, and their combined mad rushes across the water occur at intervals throughout the night. Towards morning, however, even the garrulous coots seek repose.

During April and early May reed warblers sing all night. Lapwing and redshank are heard at intervals. Snipe bleat long before sunrise; the soft whinnying sound seems doubly mysterious in the dark. Bitterns are vocally at their best an hour before sunrise. Towards dawn birds that have been singing erratically during the night become silent. There is not the regular chorus of birdsong which heralds the dawn in woodland areas; but should you have moored in the vicinity of Deep Dyke, Deep-Go-Dyke and Catfield Dyke you will catch something of the dawn chorus of the birds in the nearby woods.

After a warm night, full of mystery and pulsating with life, thin scarves of mist may suddenly float across marshes and waterways: sinuous floods which assume weird and ghostly shapes before they merge and blot out the landscape, blanketing all sound. Trees and bushes appear distorted or close at hand; landmarks

Hickling Broad from the air, looking towards the west. Whiteslea and a part of Heigham Sounds can be seen in the foreground.
Ivan West

4

Left: *Members of the reserve staff boating sedge at Hickling in 1980.*
S. Linsell

Below: *Sunset at Hill Common, Hickling.*
S. Linsell

seem to have shifted. Mental fog is apt to pervade the mind, because nothing is as it should be and a kind of wonderland exists.

Even aquatic birds are less active on misty mornings, great crested grebes being especially sluggish. They leave the sheltered margins of the reedbeds and drift down the broad with heads laid back and bodies bunched up, scarcely moving.

A sudden wave of warmth makes itself felt as the sun's red rim appears on the horizon; mists vanish, the day promises to be fine and warm, birds become lively, and you may go to sleep again if you are so inclined. It is, however, the best time of day to go pottering; so you get into a rowing boat, or better still a punt, and glide silently along the reed fringes, watching and listening, and probably annoying the inhabitants with your insatiable curiosity. There are no noisy "stink-boats" and cassette radios disturbing the wonderful peace, and you enjoy that superb feeling that the whole world belongs just to you and to the birds now awakening.

Birds are at their best when they awake, and really there is no hardship entailed in early rising on a glorious May or June morning when life is everywhere abundant. In a land of wide horizons light is quickly diffused. Birds that have been comparatively silent between their midnight orgies and dawn twitter and

Ted Ellis watches as Norman Belson tamps down a bundle of reed cut from the Hickling reedbeds.
J. Kime

call to one another. Busy parents have long considered it light enough to supply the needs of clamorous broods. Young grebes start their irritating, querulous cries, which persist all day. From the time when they are first taken out to see the world, clinging to the feathers on the nape of their parent's neck, until late autumn, when old and young leave for the sea, reservoir or river estuary, the young grebes never cease to complain.

By the middle of July the clamour of the breeding season has subsided. In fact the silence is almost uncanny, disturbed only by the peevish cries of young grebes. There are, however, other interests and excitements around the time of dawn. Waders begin to drop in. The single cry of some bird of passage may pierce the fading darkness. As August advances, the distinctive cries of green and wood sandpipers may be heard. The sharp "*chew-it, chew-it*" of a spotted redshank; the plaintive, questioning note of the grey plover; these and many other calls of migrating birds now drag the lazy observer out of bed. Later on, every day may provide a new thrill.

Although the activities of birds provide the great reason for early rising, the magic of dawn is a thing apart; beautiful and awe-inspiring at all seasons and under any conditions. A new day may call for courage; it is always an adventure. The wonder and splendour of finding oneself alive and in the company of so many feathered friends is for ever bracing.

During the last century and the early part of the present one much of what is now the nature reserve was known as the Whiteslea estate. It included most of the major waterways and the marshes and woodland along the south side of these waterways, in all an area of about 850 acres. In addition there were numerous marshes and fine mixed woods to the north-east and east of Hickling village. Some years after the purchase of the estate by Christopher Cadbury and friends in 1944, and the gift of it by them to the Norfolk Naturalists' Trust in the following year, a lease was taken by the Trust on a large area of grazing and rough marshes encompassed and bisected by dykes rich in aquatic flora, bordering the north side of the waterways. This area is still leased from Major John M. Mills. In 1957 the two areas were married together to form a sanctuary of some 1,360 acres.

Following the acquisition of the estate the famous shooting lodge at Whiteslea was leased back to Christopher Cadbury, as it still is to the present day. He has been a member of the Trust's council since 1947 and chairman of the Hickling Broad Management Committee since 1957. The reserve would not be the place it is and its facilities for visitors would not be as good as they are were it not for his great generosity over very many years.

Sony Amis of Potter Heigham at work with the grab dredger in Catfield Dyke, 1985.
S. Linsell

My first insight into this came during my early months as warden. Arthur Beales, the estate foreman, told me that the old Ferguson tractor was on its last legs, and I mentioned this to Christopher Cadbury while he was staying at Whiteslea Lodge. Some days later when he was about to leave for home he told me to order a new tractor and to forward the invoice on to him, instead of passing it to the Trust.

The visitor entering the reserve at Candle Dyke at the helm of his boat is doubtless heading either for the staithe at Hickling or for the one at Horsey. By the time he reaches either destination he might be forgiven for thinking the reserve is all water and reedbeds, but there are other habitats. There are woods, mainly of oaks and birches; areas of scrub, dominated by alder, birch, hawthorn and sallow; numerous man-made wader pools with hides; grazing marshes and areas of fen, some of them mown; within the reedswamps are dykes connecting both deep and shallow pools, miles upon miles of dykes both inside and outside the broad; and in a few places sedgebeds. Over the past thirty or forty years a marked change for the worse has overtaken many of the marshes inside the floodbank which encompasses Hickling Broad and Heigham Sounds. In order to improve the drainage of arable lands bordering these marshes the main drainage dykes are now dredged considerably deeper than they used to be, and more frequently, bringing about a lowering of the water table and a marked drying out of the marshes, which in the past were reed or sedgebeds of marketable value. As a consequence of reed and sedge not being cut for many years the seeds of bramble, alder, birch, oak and sallow have found conditions suitable for germination, and on the Potter Heigham side of the reserve woodland is now dominating what were once reed- and sedgebeds.

One of the sights which must puzzle and sadden the visitor to Hickling and Horsey is the orange-red colour of the water in some of the dykes. The dredging of drainage dykes by local drainage boards causes iron oxide, together with sulphuric acid, to be released into the water. It is iron oxide that stains the water this horrible colour. Aquatic plants become coated with the oxide for years to come and the water never clears, for after about five years the drainage board considers it is time to dredge the dykes again.

Reedbeds and large areas of fen-type habitat are no longer managed as they were during the nineteenth century and the earlier decades of the present century. Then up to sixteen men were employed at certain times of the year in reed and sedge cutting, cleaning out the dykes and mowing "litter". The latter was in great demand by London and other city stables, as well as Army cavalry barracks, for covering the floors of the stables. With the decline of this industry fen areas became neglected and were gradually invaded by trees and other vegetation, to the extent that open fens eventually became woodland.

The harvest of reed and sedge is one of the oldest industries in Broadland[2]. Common reed, *Phragmites communis*, is used in thatching and making very durable fencing screens, many of which can be seen alongside the Hickling bird-hides. Reed cutting is an arduous winter task; cutting cannot commence until about mid-December, by which time frosts and gales have removed the leaves from the reed stems. Until the advent of various machines marshmen wielded their scythes, both inside and outside the broad.

When I arrived at Hickling Mayfield self-propelled mechanical scythes had been in use for some years for cutting reed; then in my first winter the management committee decided to bring in the only Seiga reed-harvester in Britain. This is a first-class machine, for not only does it cut a broad swathe through the reeds but it bundles them and ties a string round each bundle, ready for a man standing beside the driver to pick it up and stack it on the sizable rear platform. In this way about two hundred bundles are carried to the edge of the marsh for dressing-out at a later date, leaving no accumulation of litter on the mown marsh.

The Seiga runs on four wheels, each with an enormous balloon tyre four feet wide. I always remember it arriving, and in particular recall seeing the expressions on the faces of two old marshmen, Jack and Billy Nudd, and Arthur Beales, the estate foreman and assistant warden; in a photograph I took of them they appear to be expressing their thoughts in no uncertain way!

We had the Seiga only that one time, as our reedbeds are not really vast enough to warrant the owner bringing it all the way from Scotland every winter. And there were some who thought those four huge tyres damaged the roots of the reed. In 1978 a new reed-harvester, brought over from Holland, was demonstrated on a marsh at Ranworth. Designed by some clever Japanese for harvesting rice, the machine was adapted by an enterprising chap in Holland so that it would cut reed. Like the Seiga, it cuts the reeds, bundles them and ties each bundle. Weighing almost half a

Hickling marshmen George Newman and Gerald Nudd loading sedge near Whiteslea.
S. Linsell

ton, it is so beautifully balanced that one man can operate it for long periods at a time.

Thanks to the generosity of Trust members Richard and Tavy Archer we acquired one of these Olympia harvesters during the winter of 1978–79, and what a boon it has proved to be, enabling us to produce more reed for the thatchers than was possible using the faithful old Mayfields. In a kind winter like 1980 we produced 21,700 bundles, which sold for 63 pence a bundle. Over half our production annually went to Newton Abbot in Devon for onward passage to thatchers.

Whereas reed is cut in the same areas every year, saw sedge (*Cladium mariscus*) is usually harvested on a four-yearly cycle. Being pliable, the sedge is used for the capping on thatched roofs. Comparatively little of the saw sedge grows on the reserve nowadays, and we can perhaps find two thousand bundles once every three to four years.

Modern mechanised methods of reedcutting at Hickling restrict the annual harvest to those reedbeds inside the floodbanks, and consequently our reed lighter is no longer used to transport the reeds to Hickling staithe. In the beds that fringe the main waterways the reeds can be cut only with a hand scythe, and they have not been cut for many years; they are now suffering from lack of this type of management. In the old days any area that could not

be cut was set on fire; there were plenty of men to keep the flames under control.

Some sedgebeds have also suffered, though from quite different causes. That large rodent, the coypu — an adult male measures nearly three feet from nose to tail — was first imported from its native South America in the nineteen-twenties when breeding farms were established in East Anglia for the production of the animal's fur, known in the fur trade as nutria. Many of these farms were forced to close down during the Second World War and the animals were released into the wild. These released animals found Broadland the perfect home from home and the roots and growth of sedge very appetising, and their numbers increased rapidly, for each female may have several litters a year. In addition to damaging sedgebeds the coypu burrowed into river banks and the floodbanks around the broads, and it became clear that some form of control was highly necessary. The first coypu was shot at Hickling on 1st October, 1949, and an intensive trapping campaign was later undertaken by Coypu Control. Up to the early nineteen-eighties visitors to the reserve would regularly see coypu grazing grasses and other vegetation on one or more of the wader pools, sometimes close in front of one of the hides, but by 1987 it was considered to be extinct in Broadland.

During the past three decades the whole ecology of Broadland

13

has changed, with disastrous results in most areas. A few fortunate places such as land-locked Martham South Broad have escaped, but Hickling Broad, Heigham Sounds and Horsey Mere, which once had gin-clear waters with a rich aquatic flora, have undergone a whole series of catastrophes.

Not that all the problems have arisen in recent years, for in the nineteen-thirties the local newspapers told of what they called "the Hickling Broad weed menace", and thirty years later Norfolk's best-loved naturalist, Ted Ellis, observed that a particular feature of Hickling Broad was the blanket weed (*Cladophora sauteri*), which in summer "increased to such extent as to embarrass navigators". The worst-affected areas were the channel across the broad and from Deep Dyke to Candle Dyke.

In 1933 Mr John Loynes of Wroxham, a pioneer of the holiday industry, then in his ninetieth year, devoted his remarkable energies to combating this weed menace. Men using hand dydles and lighters for transporting the weed ashore had over the

The wherry Caroline *was fitted with a steam engine and centrifugal pumps to suck out the blanket weed that choked Hickling Broad in the nineteen-thirties. The weed was deposited on the marshes by the long pipe on the left.*

Robert Malster

previous ten years cleared more than 20,000 tons at a cost of £2,000, but all their efforts had failed and the weed increased. Hickling residents observed that the weed was at its worst between 1914 and 1920, when wading birds were frequently seen "walking across the broad"[3].

Several possible solutions were thought up. Some people favoured poisoning, others suggested damming off the broad and filling it up with tons of salt. John Loynes, hearing of the possible loss of Hickling Broad as a navigable water, decided to experiment with a large dydle. He rigged his famous old yacht *Victoria* with a net fixed to the end of a boom; by hauling on the boom the net, three feet wide and three feet deep, was trawled along the bottom to scoop up the weed, which was then emptied into a lighter alongside.

So successful was John Loynes's experiment that a demonstration was given to members of the Port and Haven Commissioners in October, 1933. When asked how long he thought it would take to clear the three-mile-long channel from the head of the broad to Candle Dyke, he replied that if a wherry and two lighters, with five men, were made available he estimated six months. In due course his scheme got under way.

The weed continued to return annually, and eventually the Commissioners provided a much improved self-propelled weed dredger which worked unceasingly throughout every summer. Until, that is, man in his ignorance destroyed the aquatic flora. In 1967 the nearby Horsey Mere was dredged and, as local marshmen had correctly predicted, "the crust [the bottom of the Mere] was broken and in came saltwater", destroying the variety of water weeds not only in the Mere but in Hickling Broad and Heigham Sounds.

Since the nineteen-fifties Broadland's wildlife has been increasingly affected by the over-enrichment of the waterways by phosphates and nitrates. Some of these come from the run-off of nitrogenous fertilizer from arable land and poorly treated effluent from sewage works, but in the case of Hickling there is also a large input of phosphates from a huge roost of black-headed gulls on the main broad. These were estimated to total nearly a quarter of a million during the nineteen-seventies, but with the closure of Martham refuse tip the number of gulls, thankfully, declined to about 25,000. Even so, there must be a fair weight of guano going into the broad every night for half the year.

In 1976 the Nature Conservancy Council, the Norfolk Naturalists' Trust and the School of Environmental Sciences at the University of East Anglia decided to carry out a study of the water quality in the broad. In June the following year the NCC funded the installation of two huge butile rubber tubes, known as Lund tubes after their designer, Dr John Lund, of the Freshwater Biological Association. These tubes, floating on the surface like enormous car inner tubes, were twenty metres in diameter, and suspended beneath each tube was a rubber "skirt". Adding weight to the bottom of the skirt was about a quarter of a ton of chain which settled in the mud, effectively isolating the water within the tubes from the outside water. The hundred metres square which the tubes occupied was encompassed by a palisade of stout posts and a locked gate.

As part of the experiment, certain areas within the palisade had netting laid into the sediment to stabilize it, while others were left clear. Some of these areas were regularly disturbed with a motorboat, others were protected from all boat action.

Students from the University in Norwich came out two or three times a week throughout the months the experiment lasted, bringing with them a rubber dinghy with outboard motor which was launched at the Pleasure Boat staithe. As the monitoring of the experiments continued into autumn and winter, the students were baffled as to why the phosphate content in the water enclosed by both tubes steadily increased, while that in the broad remained fairly constant. Then one night in December at the period of full moon, and in perfect weather conditions, I took a punt out round the waterways. When I reached Heigham Corner I found black-headed gulls standing shoulder to shoulder all round both tubes, all facing outwards; they were dropping phosphate into the water within the tubes as they roosted there throughout the night. The following summer the whole area was netted over, which put an end to this problem.

The experiments produced a number of critical findings. Firstly, protection from boat disturbance within the palisade did not increase the growth of aquatic plants; they do cope quite well with mechanical damage. Secondly, plants grew better in the areas enclosed by the tubes, where the relative absence of nutrients from roosting birds and of water pumped from the catchment area led to lesser growth of algae on the plant leaves. And thirdly, although the phytoplankton in the water within the tubes became very short of nutrients, it persisted in quantity because it was not grazed very much by zooplankton. In turn the numbers of a water shrimp, *Neomysis*, which probably feeds on the zooplankton, were high because these themselves were not being eaten by fish. The fish stock was kept low by *Prymnesium*, but more about this in a moment.

All in all the results of these Lund tube experiments showed that a complex situation exists in Hickling Broad. They have helped to improve very much our ideas on how some of the broads have changed and what we ought to do to restore them.

Because of the over-enrichment of the waters in the broad, in

Heigham Sounds, and in all the dykes running off them, they have become like pea soup, due to the massive proliferation of minute algae. Owing to the shallowness of these waterways the water warms up rapidly from late May onwards, and the warmer the water becomes the more abundantly do the algae multiply. In most years, by mid-July a white disc cannot be seen three inches below the surface. To this pea soup we must add the silt constantly stirred up by the daily passage of dozens of boats. At times of low water a blackish slick marks the wake of most boats, whose propellers are turning either in the silt or just above it. The resulting turbidity prevents sunlight reaching any plants, or their seeds, which may still exist, and without light they cannot grow.

At the end of every summer the waters cool down and the algae die, to settle on the silt below, thereby causing another problem, an increase in sedimentation. We are told by those monitoring silting in various parts of Broadland that a centimetre or more of silt is being deposited annually.

Further pressures have been exerted on the broads and connecting rivers and dykes by an ever-increasing number of powerboats. There are some 125 miles of navigable waterways available for tourism and recreation, and these have to accommodate many thousands of boats at the peak of the holiday season. Rather more than two thousand cruisers, both power and sailing, are available for hire weekly. Some five hundred self-drive launches can also be hired by day visitors from a few boatyards. In addition to these tourist craft it is said there are nearly eight thousand privately-owned boats licensed to use the waterways.

Some thoughtless hirers of cruisers, as well as a few private owners, have been known to drive their vessels into riverside reedbeds and the reedbeds bordering some broads, doubtless unaware of the damage they do to fauna and flora. Not only is the plant life damaged, but a coot, a moorhen, a reed warbler, or some other bird may have built its nest at that very spot.

It is not only we humans who bring pressures on the broads, for Nature can take a hand also. Many of the reedbeds surrounding broads such as Hickling are basically large floating mattresses, and the action of waves raised by storm-force winds on these cause "hovers", pieces normally about the size of a dining-room table but sometimes much larger, to break away. They ultimately finish up against some leeward shore.

Occasionally one finds a really large hover, such as the one that broke free in Deep Dyke on the night of 13th January, 1981. A great piece of the reedbed on the north side came adrift and, held fast at one end, swung across this wide dyke and jammed itself against the opposite bank. Access to the broad or off it was impossible.

Meadow Dyke, leading from Heigham Sounds to Horsey Mere, showing on the left bank erosion resulting from the loss of reedswamp. S. Linsell

On another wild night a huge hover broke away from the south side of Heigham Sounds and eventually fetched up against Potter Heigham Bridge, completely blocking it. Our reserve staff cut the hover up into smaller pieces and helped to tow them back to the Sounds.

There is evidence that enrichment of the waters by phosphates and nitrates is the main reason for the disappearance of the reedswamp, although other factors such as the grazing and trampling of the vegetation by ever-increasing hordes of Canada and greylag geese, and the grazing by coypu in the past, undoubtedly contribute to the problem. The phenomenon known as reedswamp "dieback" is of the utmost importance because it causes a major change in the ecology of the waterways. In the rivers it also leads to a substantial increase in bank erosion caused by the wash of passing boats; the boats themselves cause damage when moored against the reedswamp.

A classic example of all these effects on reedswamp can be seen between the River Thurne and Hickling Broad, particularly in Candle Dyke. Along the south side the reeds have nearly all gone, while on the north side the reedswamp which until the early nineteen-seventies completely isolated Duck Broad from Candle Dyke will probably all be gone in another ten years or so.

In some places such as Deep Dyke, which has always been one of the best fishing waters for bream, a minority of fishermen have contributed to the decay of the reedswamp. I must stress that it is no more than a minority, but the offending anglers bring with them not only their fishing tackle but a machete or slasher of some kind, and when they cannot find a stretch of vegetation-free bank to fish from they slash down the plants, even cutting small trees to ensure that hook and line do not get caught up when they cast.

The result along the south side of Deep Dyke just before you enter the broad was a bare bank of unsupported peat, at the mercy of wave action from passing boats; the once-natural fringe of reeds, reedmace and other plants had completely disappeared. Here during the winter of 1981 the River Commissioners were forced to quayhead 600 feet of the bank with sheets of galvanized steel.

The reader might think after reading such a catalogue of catastrophes that there cannot be more gloomy stories to tell, but most unhappily this does not end the list of natural and man-made disasters. Two quite natural poisons have caused havoc in the Hickling area in recent years, in one case killing great numbers of birds and in the other decimating the fish population.

In the deposits of silt on the bottom of most of the broads exists a bacterium, *Clostridium botulinum*, which proliferates during warm sunny weather and produces a toxin responsible for outbreaks of avian botulism. In the case of birds botulism causes the wings to become paralysed, then the legs and finally the head and the neck. That superb summer of 1976 saw botulism at its worst: throughout Broadland thousands of waterfowl and gulls and unknown numbers of wading birds died.

At Hickling a fenced-off pen was made in our garden where sick birds like the ruff, redshank, ringed plover, lapwing, and green and wood sandpipers were put. Many died, but some, like one wood sandpiper which I had picked up with only the wings affected, had water trickled down their throats several times daily and recovered. I remember this wood sandpiper particularly, for the day came when this bird could fly again and I released it on one of the wader pools. For some time it fed hungrily, and then took flight. As it disappeared southwards above Whiteslea I prayed it was strong enough to complete its migration to Africa.

In 1969 the alga *Prymnesium parvum* appeared in the waters of Hickling and Horsey. This particular alga is capable of liberating toxins into the water and thereby greatly reducing the oxygen content, resulting in numerous disastrous fish-kills, none worse than that first one in 1969, when many tons of dead fish were removed from the waterways. Since that time these two northern broads as well as Heigham Sounds have ceased to be Britain's top pike fishing waters. I have noticed that when *Prymnesium* occurs it is always pike that die first, but I have not found more than a dozen or so annually, these weighing between four and ten pounds.

And yet another gloomy story! Sailing across Hickling Broad any year in the nineteen-sixties or earlier one would see four hundred of our native swans. What a superb sight they were, and how they brought the broad to life. Their progress was slow, for they had to force their way through the water lilies, marestail, water milfoil and other aquatic plants thriving in the crystal-clear water.

> Where the wash of Hickling waters
> Lap the sides of grassy bank,
> Where phragmites tall and slender
> Grows with marsh grass thick and lank.
>
> When you stand upon the look-out
> And t'wards Catfield Dyke you gaze,
> Such a herd of swans you see there
> All amidst the morning haze.
>
> Stuart Boardman

Since 1970, however, the swans have virtually gone. In most years no more than three or four pairs nest among the reedbeds, and in 1985 only one pair nested on this 1,360-acre reserve. Most of the plants have gone, and swans being vegetarians have been forced to go elsewhere for food.

Some of those which stayed have died from lead poisoning, having swallowed lead weights left around by anglers. Others have choked to death through swallowing "hook, line, and sinker". Now and then during the winter I have come across pochard and tufted duck floating dead against the reed fringes, killed by swallowing hook or line or becoming entangled in line and having starved to death. Now that lead weights are, officially, a thing of the past waterfowl may cease to die from this source of lead poisoning, but some will continue to die because nylon line is left lying around. One can only repeat warnings to anglers of the danger of discarding tackle.

We must not blame only a minority of anglers for the presence of lead pellets on and around Hickling Broad and elsewhere in Broadland. For over a hundred years wildfowlers poured a fair tonnage of lead shot into the waterways, where it sank into the mud and silt beneath a mattress of aquatic plants. Swans found this mattress of plants difficult to penetrate; indeed there was no reason for them to do so, for there was an abundance and variety of food plants on or near the surface. Now that this dense aquatic flora has disappeared swans can reach the silt and the lead shot in it. Over the past two decades scores of our native swans have died throughout Broadland from lead poisoning. Many were picked up either dead or very sick by myself or by Len Baker and his staff from the wonderful Swan Rescue Service, founded by Len and his wife Sheilah.

One may well ask what steps are being taken to improve water quality and to restore Broadland to its former glory. Certainly some steps have been taken by the Nature Conservancy Council and the Broads Authority to encourage farmers either to maintain age-old grazing marshes and not to convert them to arable use or to restore to grazing those marshes that had gone under the plough before the existing financial incentives came into force. The Broads Authority has made a start in restoring some broads by damming them off from polluted rivers and removing the noxious layers of silt with a mud pump; one only has to visit Cockshoot Broad to see how effective this has been. And Anglian Water have made a start on reducing the amount of phosphates leaving some of their sewage works.

Around the broads and adjacent to rivers and dykes various conservation bodies and individuals are doing their bit to restore neglected reed- and sedgebeds, as well as areas of fen. And the never-ending task of clearing marshes of scrub goes on relentlessly.

What might well turn out to be one of the most significant developments of all for the Broads came about on 1st April, 1989, when the new Broads Authority took charge of the region's future restoration and wellbeing. To all intents and purposes, though not in name, Broadland then came a national park.

With such changes taking place it was natural that television companies and similar organizations should take an interest in the Broads, and during my time at Hickling it was not uncommon to

A working party from Martham West Flegg Middle School receiving instruction in scrub clearing from warden Stewart Linsell.
Eastern Daily Press

receive telephone calls from the BBC, Anglia Television or one of the other ITV companies saying that they wanted to do some filming on the broad, and "Can we have the use of your reed lighter and someone to drive it?" With its shallow draught and wide beam, and its stability, it is the perfect boat for filming.

During most years some television company or other has come to film the harvests of reed and sedge. I was particularly pleased when in 1986 an ITV film unit came to make a documentary of Hickling marshmen George Newman and Gerald Nudd harvesting sedge near Whiteslea and boating it to the Pleasure Boat Inn staithe.

It was not only the television companies that came. The first filming took place on Hickling in the summer of 1952, when many sequences were shot for that delightful film "A Conflict Of Wings", starring John Gregson, Muriel Pavlow and Kieron Moore. Pleasure Island in the broad played its part as the site of a bombing range which the RAF were determined to use despite much spirited opposition from local inhabitants. Many of Hickling's residents took part as "extras". Scenes were also shot for "The Go-Between", starring Alan Bates and Julie Christie, and some of the filming of "The Life of Sir Ernest Shackleton" was done at Miss Turner's Island; Sir Ernest and his wife had spent their honeymoon on the Broads. In 1985 great fun was had by one and all in filming sequences for "Swallows and Amazons".

Not every filming session was successful, however. During the nineteen-seventies a BBC television crew came to the broad with the intention of doing some underwater filming of plant life and were taken out in the reed lighter, which can get to the shallowest of waters; they took one look at the pea-soup conditions and realized that filming at Hickling was out of the question. At the suggestion of Peter Stevens, the Trust's conservation officer at the time, they were taken to Martham Broad, where with the assistance of Frank Pigg, the warden, they obtained some excellent film of underwater plant life in its clear waters.

Despite all these gloomy tales about the present state of the waters in Hickling Broad, I can at least give the botanist a note of comfort. One of the rarest submerged water plants in Britain, the holly-leaved naiad *Naias marina*, manages to survive in one or two secluded areas where it does not get chopped up by boat propellers. It was first recorded in Hickling Broad in 1883, and was unknown elsewhere in Britain until the nineteen-fifties, when it was found in four other broads. In just one quiet backwater in 1986 I found a few examples of the shining pondweed *Potomogeton lucens*, and there was a time, not so very long ago, when pochard weed, *Nitellopsis obtusa*, thrived in Hickling Broad, its only known site in England.

Right: *A wood sandpiper suffering from botulism, which causes paralysis and ultimately kills. This particular bird, picked up with the wings paralysed, survived to begin its migration flight to Africa.* S. Linsell

Below: *The flooding of grazing marshes in autumn attracts wildfowl and waders to the reserve. This marsh at Hickling is part of The Hundred Acres.* S. Linsell

In the Past 2

A S THE holidaymaker steers a course up the River Bure from Great Yarmouth and thence into the River Thurne bound for Hickling Broad, he probably has no idea that a couple of thousand years ago the North Sea covered much of the land he now sees. At the time of the Roman occupation a vast estuary, with its north and south headlands at Caister and Burgh Castle, extended inland as far as Norwich, Bungay and Aylsham. This huge stretch of inland water, known as the Sea of Gariensis, was almost five miles wide at its mouth; all that remains today is Breydon Water, a relatively small area of tidal water behind Great Yarmouth.

North of Caister was another opening through which the tides ebbed and flowed at Horsey. Even today a ridge of denes or sand dunes, tentatively held together by marram grass, is all that separates the pounding waves from the marshlands around Hickling Broad and Horsey Mere. Over the centuries severe erosion of the coast between Cromer and Happisburgh (pronounced Haisbro) brought about the formation of sandbanks across the mouth of the Sea of Gariensis, on which fishermen established the settlement of wooden huts that eventually grew into the town of Great Yarmouth. As more and more sand and silt was deposited the entrance to the estuary narrowed steadily.

The Romans built a large walled town at Caister and a massive fort at Burgh, where a sizable fleet was based in readiness to repel the feared Saxon warriors. We learn from historians that in the ninth century the Danes often ravaged the Norfolk coast, and dwellers on the shores of the Sea of Gariensis suffered severely at their hands; in 1004 Sweyn led a Danish fleet up to Norwich, which he plundered and burned.

About the year 500 an Anglo-Saxon village existed at Hicel, as Hickling was then known; *Hicel* being Anglo-Saxon for "a place near a meadow". About 450 years later the Danes called the village Hiceling, their word *ing* meaning people, hence "people of a place near a meadow".

Historians investigating the origin of the broads and the effects of changes of sea level on the Norfolk coast have found evidence that East Anglia has see-sawed up and down over the past four thousand years as a result of the melting of the ice which covered so much of the land during the last Ice Age. The effect of

The view of Hickling Broad seen from the lookout at Whiteslea Lodge, the roof of which can be seen in the foreground. This superb view has been captured on canvas by many a famous artist. S. Linsell

25

the thaw was very much that of a man's weight being removed from a small boat as he steps ashore; the boat rocks to and fro in a gradually decreasing cycle[1].

Immediately after 2000 BC the sea flooded in as the land fell; then the land rose, reaching its highest point about 1000 BC before falling again to produce a rather greater marine transgression in early Romano-British times which resulted in the formation of the Sea of Gariensis. The waters drained away again as the land emerged once more, reaching a peak about AD 700. There is evidence from deep excavations made at Great Yarmouth that at the time of the Norman Conquest the land was at least 13 feet higher than it is now, the present level being the result of a steady submergence which has continued up to the present.

Researchers into the origins of the broads found abundant evidence of an important turf or peat industry in east Norfolk at least as early as the tenth century. Man dug peat for fuel; he warmed his home by it and he cooked by it. And an establishment like the important monastery at Norwich annually purchased some 400,000 turves of peat, at a cost, as we read in the monastic records, of about twelve pounds[2].

The early peat diggers would have had no difficulty in extracting the turves, in spite of the fact that the best combustible peat was found three feet and more below the surface, because the sea level was low and the peat beds were well above water. The peat beds were shallowest in the Hickling–Horsey area and became progressively deeper towards the south of the county. The peat diggings which ultimately formed Hickling Broad were no more than four feet deep, but those which resulted in the formation of

Two maps by Dr J. M. Lambert showing Hickling Broad, Whiteslea and Heigham Sounds in 1840–42 and 1946. The diminution of open water is clearly apparent. From E. A. Ellis: *The Broads*

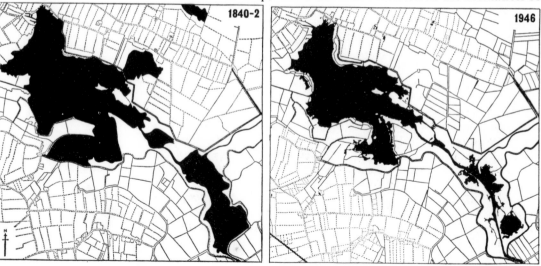

Fritton Lake must have reached a greater depth; Fritton Lake today is about 16 feet deep.

Over the centuries the peat diggers created pits large and small, deep and shallow, which became flooded as the land fell and water levels rose. Thus were the broads formed. Many of the broads were eventually connected with the river system by man-made dykes; one of the longest of these is Meadow Dyke, connecting Horsey Mere with Heigham Sounds.

It has been my experience that the majority of holidaymakers visiting Hickling are quite unaware of the origin of the broads, which they assume to be merely widenings of the rivers. In fact the broads lie away from the main rivers, as one would expect of former peat cuttings. J. W. Gregory made this point emphatically in 1892, when he wrote:

> Instead of the river passing through the broads, it kept sullenly aloof from them; as we sailed down the river there was broad to the left of us, broad to the right of us, broad in front of us, but by a series of ingenious twists and turns it managed to wind through the whole lot of them, either eluding any direct contact with them or communicating only by a few narrow and overgrown passages.[3]

As the land fell and the waters correspondingly flowed into the peat pits and over the lower-lying land in late medieval times efforts were made to keep the waters out and eventually to drain some of the swampy marshes. Rivers were embanked and causeways constructed across treacherous fens, but for centuries there remained wide tracts of swamp where the bittern, avocet, ruff, spoonbill and black tern nested and over which buzzards soared.

The rise in sea level did not entirely stop the digging of peat, for my own experience has shown that it is possible to dig peat to a depth of several feet provided the area is isolated from tidal flooding, even though the water table is only a foot or two below the surface of the fen. An ornamental swimming pool was excavated in the Hickling marshes to a depth of more than eight feet entirely by hand labour without the use of pumps, with the men working well below the level of water in the nearby dykes.

Peat was not the only material dug from the ground in these parts. Whereas Hickling Broad was created as a result of peat digging, Heigham Sounds evolved through the digging of the estuarine clay laid down during an earlier marine transgression. The clay was used in the making of bricks and pottery.

The Black Death in 1349, which killed 50,000 people in Norwich and 7,000 in Great Yarmouth, did not leave Hickling unaffected. Brought from overseas by some ship from an infected continental port, the plague first attacked the coastal towns before spreading along the river valleys from one village to the next. At

Hickling Priory, founded by Theobald de Valoins in 1185, only one canon survived. It is impossible to visualize the horrors of that awful summer. Beside the rivers flowing sluggishly through desolate swamps stood fine buildings, churches and nunneries that were destined to become centres of contagion. People fled from stricken villages and towns to these sanctuaries, believing that their only hope of escaping the plague lay there. But they brought the Black Death with them, and died there in their hundreds[4].

In the late sixteenth century Dutch settlers arrived at Yarmouth. Experts in land reclamation, they were probably responsible for some of the embanking of the rivers and broads. It is possible that the floodbanks which contain the waters of Hickling Broad and Heigham Sounds were constructed by Dutch engineers. Before this the area of these waterways extended to over a thousand acres, more than double that of the present day. Since the construction work was completed reedswamp has colonized large areas, especially in Heigham Sounds, which has only a fraction of its previous water area.

While efforts were being made to drain the swamps, the sea still tried hard to win back its ancient bed; occasionally it succeeded. The fragile barrier of sand dunes at Horsey has been breached with catastrophic results about once each century. The earliest account can be read in the chronicles of John of Oxnead, quoted by William Dutt in *The Norfolk Broads*:

In 1287, in the month of December, the seventh of the Kalends of January, the 8th day of the moon, the sea, in dense darkness, began to be agitated by the violence of the wind, and in its agitation to burst through its accustomed limits, occupying towns, fields and other places adjacent to the coast, and inundating parts which no age in past times had recorded to have been covered with sea water. For, issuing forth about the middle of the night, it suffocated or drowned men and women sleeping in their beds, with infants in their cradles, and all kinds of cattle and fresh-water fishes; and it tore up houses from their foundations with all they contained, and carried them away and threw them into the sea with irrecoverable damage. Many, when surrounded by the waters, sought a place of refuge by mounting into trees; but, benumbed by the cold, they were overtaken by the water and fell into it and were drowned. Whereby it happened that in the town of Hyckelyngge [Hickling] nine score of different sexes and ages perished in the aforesaid inundation.

Even this disaster was surpassed by the devastation caused in 1607 when sea defences collapsed and seawater flooded areas of Kent, Essex, Suffolk and Norfolk; for then, we are told, thousands of men, women and children were drowned, whole towns and villages demolished, and vast numbers of cattle and sheep destroyed. So serious was this damage that Parliament in 1609 passed an Act "for the speedy recovery of many thousands of acres of Marsh Ground and other Ground within the Counties of Norfolk and Suffolk, lately surrounded by the Rage of the sea in divers parts of the said Counties, and for the Prevention of Danger of the like surrounding hereafter". The sea, we are informed by the preamble of this Act, had caused a flood affecting places between Horsey and Gillingham and as far inland as Norwich. At Great Yarmouth part of the Haven Bridge was destroyed, and the Haven House, in which were the "Haven man" and his son, was "carried into the marshes six miles from the Haven"[5].

The eighteenth-century Norfolk historian the Rev. Francis Blomefield, writing of the 1609 Act, tells us that to prevent such inundations by the sea occurring again, "there were appointed eighteen commissioners, who, according to the direction of the Act, were to stop the breaches, it being to be feared that in time to come further mischief might follow by other breaches, or enlarging of

Staithe Road, Hickling, flooded after the sea had broken through at Horsey Gap in 1938.
per M. Belson

those already made, if speedy remedy be not provided, and God of His mercy stop not the same". Nevertheless, despite Man's efforts over the centuries to keep the sea out, there have been other disastrous floods, most recent being those of 1938 and 1953.

I remember seeing the effects of the 1938 flood, for not long after it happened the headmaster at Bishop's Stortford College took a party of us boys to the school's "holiday farm" at Happisburgh. Between Sea Palling and Horsey and southwards throughout a large part of Hickling parish there was utter devastation of the land, people's gardens killed outright, hedges and trees destroyed by salt water, and everywhere dead fish. For a first-hand detailed description of this flood we cannot do better than refer to the writings of Major Anthony Buxton, who resided at Horsey Hall at that time:

As the result of a great north-west gale, which coincided with full moon, we were subjected in February, 1938, to a sea flood which, entering by a breach in the sand-hills half a mile wide, covered an area of 7,500 acres including the whole parish of Horsey with the exception of an island of 120 acres and a narrow strip consisting of the sand-hills and a belt just inland from them. This disaster was the latest of a long series that have occurred on the dangerous coast between Winterton and Happisburgh.

The earliest breach, of which historical record exists, was in 1287, when one hundred and eight persons were drowned in Hickling alone. The more recent breaches occurred in 1792, 1805 and 1897. In 1938 the sea water covered an area of 7,500 acres, most of it for a period of three months. Since such a phenomenon is fortunately rare in this country, and since its effects are little understood, some account shall be given of what occurred at the time and of the slow process of recovery that succeeded it.

At about 7.30 p.m on the evening of February 12, 1938, a farmer came into my house with the news, "The sea is in," and I ran out to find, within about 150 yards of the house, the sea on the road, a mass of dead earthworms floating about and terrified hares and rabbits swimming in or galloping before the flood. I waded to the millman's house and at my knock he stepped straight out of his door into the sea. We were in time to rescue some people in a boat from the upper windows of their house and to get some of the inhabitants of the village away in a lorry down the road to the north, two of us wading through the sea down the road ahead of the lorry, holding the centre of the road by keeping an eye on the tops of the reeds that showed in the dykes on either side of us. Except at one gateway there was no great current, but we had the feeling of complete ignorance as to how high the water would rise. Luckily a bright moon helped us, for we could at least see what was happening. There was luckily no loss of human life and little loss of farm animals. Horses and cattle, which in many cases were standing out for hours belly-deep in the sea with nothing to eat but dead floating rubbish and no fresh water to drink, took the ordeal with great calmness and showed no inclination to stampede. All fresh water fish

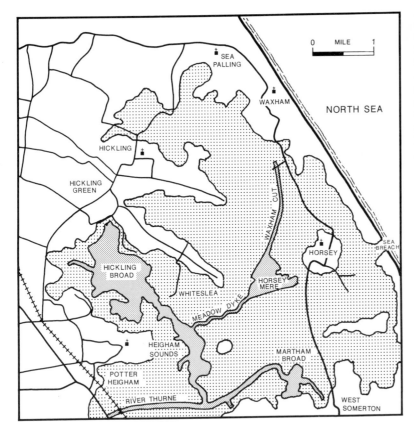

were at once destroyed and floated in thousands on the water; there was of course an invasion of the inhabitants of the sea. The only creatures which appeared quite unaffected were the eels, whose habit of migrating from sea water to fresh and back again made them apparently indifferent to what had occurred.

For the next three months until the half-mile breach in the sand-hills was sealed we lived a strange existence on an island at the mercy of the sea, with the water rising and falling according to the tide and to the force and direction of the wind. The normal drainage system of the country was completely upset, for the water on the land rose above the level of the walls surrounding the broads and rivers and flowed over the walls into them. Luckily at the moment of the breach the rivers were not particularly full and much of the sea water that entered at the breach flowed away down the rivers and re-entered the sea at Yarmouth without any action by man. If this had not been the case far more land would have been covered by sea water. We tried, whenever the water dropped an inch or two in the rivers, to assist this natural process by cutting slits in the walls bordering the rivers and broads to let some

31

water off the land, but constantly had to re-close these slits whenever the water in the rivers rose again. All such work was really wasted and it was useless to do anything before the breach was closed, which took three months to accomplish.

For those three months, the sea lay on the land, and pumps and all other contraptions were useless, but once the breach was enclosed, engines and windmills worked day and night and thanks to the millmen the water was pumped off the land down to the level of the dykes in another six weeks. The final scene was a strange one. A mass of sea water, thick and yellow, poured through the dykes to the pumping stations where it was pumped into the rivers and broads. This flood took with it every form of rubbish and a mass of sea fish, which, swirled and battered by the machinery, were pounced upon by a mass of gulls collected for the feast. Herrings, grey mullet, sprats, shrimps, crabs (my keeper saw a crab walk across a ploughed field), and other creatures of the sea were the only inhabitants of the flood and they were all eventually destroyed or swept back to their proper home via Yarmouth. Barnacles swarmed on the reed stems and on debris in Horsey Mere, where they survived until the first frost of the following winter, but marine shrimps remained in large quantities for at least three years and were a special attraction to certain birds, in particular to spotted crakes. The destruction of rats and mice naturally caused the departure of the hawks and owls, and the destruction of vegetation, insects, and other forms of life, caused the departure of other birds.

An inland sea that turned into a desert was my general impression of the flood, and its worst feature was the resulting lack of life. There was some beauty in the scene, particularly at sunrise and sunset, while the water covered the land; there was none in the aftermath. The boundary line between flooded and unflooded area was during the spring and summer blatantly abrupt—from bright green life to red-brown death: it was reminiscent of an impressionist picture and a bad one at that, and over all hung the smell of a stale salting. Perhaps the worst feature of all was the dead timber, standing stark and bare of leaves, growing as time went on more skeleton-like as the bark stripped from the stems, and left them bare and glistening.

As the first autumn came depression began to give way to interest. Things began to happen, life in peculiar forms and ways began to creep back. A little grass and other seedlings appeared on the sides of the roads and at the feet of trees where fresh water dripped, fat hen (*Chenopodium album*), the forerunner of the goosefoot incursion, which was to be one of the main early features in recovery, came up all over the place, to be followed by its cousin orach (*Atriplex patula*), which sprawled luxuriantly in plants ten feet across about high-water mark, while beet, the other member of that salt-loving family, appeared as isolated plants in all directions on marsh or arable and in woods, wherever the seed had been deposited by the sea and subsequently germinated. Samphire or edible sea-weed (*Salicornia Europaea*) covered the marshes. Throughout the period of recovery from the earliest stages there were constant instances of the ability of seed to withstand the salted conditions and to germinate as soon as salinity had dropped

Stubb Mill, Hickling, at work in 1930.
per Billy Nudd

to the required degree. The ability of seed to hibernate until the right moment and then to germinate is understandable. The ability of bulbs to do the same thing is more difficult to understand, but it exists. In the autumn of 1937 a mixed lot of daffodil bulbs were planted in a wood, which was covered by the sea in February, 1938, for 100 days. Nothing whatever was seen of the daffodils either in the shape of leaves or flowers until the spring of 1945, when a considerable number appeared and flowered really well. Those bulbs had remained dormant for eight years and then had shown full vigour.[6]

I have been fortunate in obtaining first-hand knowledge of how Hickling was affected by this flood from the man who first knew about it—Billy Nudd, who has lived at Stubb Mill all his eighty-two years, and has been millman there all his working life. Fortunately the village itself escaped inundation, but only because

A group looking at the foaming of the floodwater as it is pumped off the marshes by Stubb Mill. Billy Nudd stands with Mrs Ian Thomson on the right; the others are Jimmy Newman, Jack Thaine and six-year-old Tom Nudd.
per Billy Nudd

Left: *Fish killed by the saltwater during the 1938 sea floods; only the eels were unaffected by the salinity.* per Billy Nudd

Below: *Stubb Mill outfall; the mill was no longer worked by the wind and a steam engine was used to turn the scoopwheel.*
per Billy Nudd

of the tremendous efforts of many of the men of the parish, as Billy
Nudd recalls:

On February 12th, 1938, a Saturday night, without any warning, flood
water appeared in the Stubb Mill outlet at higher levels than I had ever
seen before. On looking out at this from the bedroom window on the
Sunday morning, I realized something had to be done as water was
coming over the bank. I took a spade along the outlet wall, where I
knew there was a low place, and to my surprise that low place was about
100 yards long and water was coming over to a depth of about one foot.
Realizing I could not possibly tackle this on my own, I returned home
for a quick breakfast, then cycled up the road to call at all nearby houses
and to ask all available menfolk to come along with spades to help fill
the breach.

This was dealt with in reasonable time with all my helpers, by
digging out spits of soil from the higher points. We then proceeded
along the banks to other low places, dealing with these in similar
manner. At this stage a village lad named Jack Thaine arrived. He had a
small boat which he kept close to mine at the Mill, and he said he was
taking it home because Hickling would be flooded out. I told him not to
be so stupid, to go and get a spade, and report to the Council Houses to
ask as many as possible to come with spades to help out, and also spread
the news that further help was urgently needed. A lot of help arrived
fairly quickly, and we then worked our way along the bank of Horsey
Wall towards Eastfield Mill, stopping the water along the way. We
reached Eastfield Mill at dusk. All of this work was carried out without

*Another view of the foam
stretching down the dyke
from the mill outfall, an
object of curiosity to local
people at the time.*
per Billy Nudd

pausing for either food or drink. Other men were working in the Whiteslea/Hickling Broad area to stem the flow of water from that quarter.

I am sure that our efforts on that Sunday saved the village of Hickling from being badly flooded. Jim Vincent called on me on the Sunday evening, saying what a good job had been done and asking if I had told the men to come next day (Monday). I replied "yes", so he said he would get some men along as well. A fresh start was made on the Monday, this time with the help of a couple of boats. We also had lots of bags, which we needed to fill up to help breach the holes in the banks. We found that planks and timber were needed, also, to help support the bags. Fortunately, we were able to lay our hands on these quickly—taking posts and planks from the fencing around us. This work continued through the whole of that week until the Friday, by which time the water had started to recede.

Jim Vincent sent me a note by messenger, asking if I thought the position was safe enough to release most of the men, but to keep just the two with the boats, who would keep an eye on the situation. He asked, also, would I call on him on the Saturday, lunchtime, with my book in which I had listed the names and times of the men who had worked, and collect the money from him to pay them. They were all paid on the Saturday night, at the rate of six shillings per day.

The outside water by this time was down low enough for me to raise steam and to get the mill working. A traction engine drove the mill's water-wheel, and had done for several years. The mill worked continuously, day and night, for five weeks, I taking care of most of the night shifts, with help on shift work during the days from Arthur Dove and Jack Riseborough. At the end of that time, thankfully, the water on the marshes was down to normal levels. I would estimate that at the height of the flooding over 1,000 acres had been affected, from a few inches up to eighteen inches; but fortunately little or no arable land was involved. Most of the marshes in the Whiteslea area were flooded to various depths.

The Hickling area was not affected by the flooding in January, 1953, which caused such damage and some loss of life at nearby Sea Palling. This time the flood banks around Hickling were not breached.

In the nineteenth century the Broads area was inhabited by men who found their living in wild places among the waterways. Every marshman lived by his gun, his eel spear and his nets. Common birds would find their way into the pot or the oven, but there was always the chance of killing a rarity which would find a ready market among the collectors, men who eagerly sought birds which could be stuffed by the taxidermist and set up in a glass case in what was considered a realistic pose.

Some of the collectors were not content to depend on the local wildfowlers but came shooting themselves, for with the advent of the railways the remotest parts of the Norfolk coastline were opened up to the "foreigner". One such "foreigner" was Edward Thomas Booth, who was born in 1840 of wealthy parents and seems to have spent his life shooting birds and stuffing them. From his early adult days his dream was to form a collection of birds set up in their natural surroundings; he was the first person to exhibit not merely a collection of stuffed birds but rather a display that provided a true representation of birds in their haunts. Eventually the authorities at the Natural History Museum in South Kensington worthily imitated his example.

One of Booth's favourite hunting grounds was the Broads, and in particular Hickling. He seems to have stayed regularly at Hickling from 1870 to about 1885, and he undoubtedly had the shooting rights for many seasons. His *Rough Notes*, published from 1881 to 1887, contain a number of references to the bittern, though Booth rarely saw one of these birds himself. He tells us:

> From the Hickling keeper, now over 70 years of age, I learnt that in his remembrance this species nested regularly in the marsh and on the hills round Hickling and several of the other broads.

Booth also mentions that in those days bearded tits' eggs fetched four shillings a dozen and that the local marshmen found nearly all the first clutches at Hickling. Ruffs were nesting there in 1870, and Booth says that he occasionally met with the eggs or broods of the spotted crake. He saw a gadwall twice at Hickling, but never discovered the nest of the pintail.

He filled up room after room in his house at Brighton with his specimens, and in 1874 acquired a property on Dyke Road, Brighton, and built himself both a new house and an adjoining museum. By the time of his death on 8th February, 1890, his collection of stuffed birds totalled 229 species, many of which were exhibited in several different stages of plumage; in all the collection occupied 308 cases. By his will he gave the museum and the collection it contained to the Corporation of Brighton "on the express understanding that they will not alter the interior of the cases, and that they will take the same care of them as he has hitherto done".

A few years before Edward Booth took an interest in Hickling Broad and its marshes a primitive cottage, undoubtedly used as a shooting lodge, stood close by Whiteslea Broad, between Hickling Broad and Heigham Sounds. The only means of access to it was by boat, or by walking a mile and a half from Hickling village along the marsh tracks. Research into deeds and other documents has shown that the Micklethwait family owned some seven thousand acres of land and water, divided between estates at Taverham and

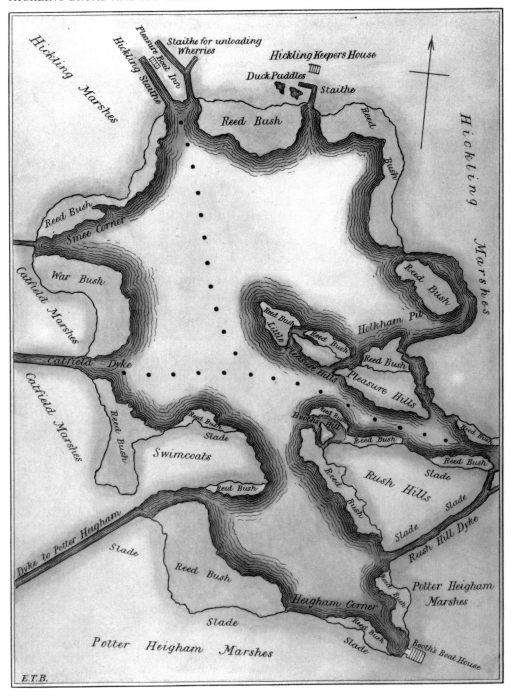

Hickling, from the mid-eighteen-twenties onwards, and the cottage must have stood on Micklethwait land. The Hickling estate consisted of Hickling Broad, Whitlesea Broad and Heigham Sounds, plus a considerable acreage of land to the north and south of these stretches of water.

The cottage is reputed to have been burned to the ground in 1861, but by 1875 a timber-built cottage with a boathouse and a shed had replaced it on the same site. In that year the cottage was conveyed to William Butcher the younger of Potter Heigham by James Duff. In succeeding years the lease of the cottage changed hands several times, and in April, 1902, it was conveyed by Ernest Connor to John Boning, who also held the shooting rights. Since that time the story of the cottage has been intertwined with the story of Hickling in a way that its original occupiers would probably have considered unlikely.

Following the death in 1901 of Major George Nathaniel Micklethwait, who had no children, the estate passed through his eldest sister Sarah Charlotte to her son, the Rev. Cecil Mills, who lived on the family estate at Bisterne in Hampshire. When he died in 1908 the estates passed to his son, Colonel John Mills.

During the time Major Micklethwait owned the estate it was keepered by Robert (Bob) Vincent, who lived in Hickling village. In 1884 Bob Vincent and his wife Rebecca had a son, whom they called Jim. Sixteen-year-old Jim was engaged in 1900 by the Hon. Edwin Montagu, a Cambridge undergraduate, to assist him in building up his collection of birds and their eggs.

That was the beginning of a link which was to prove vital to the future of Hickling Broad. Edwin Montagu, who spent much of his youth travelling the world in search of rare birds and their eggs, came back to Hickling in 1908 with a fellow bird-enthusiast, Lord Lucas, and a year later they were joined by Sir Edward Grey, who was then Foreign Secretary; he was later to become Lord Grey of Falloden, and is still remembered by birdlovers for his delightful book *The Charm of Birds*.

The three of them decided to purchase that part of the Hickling estate consisting of the southern half of the broad, Whiteslea and Heigham Sounds, plus the marshes and woods bordering the south side of the waterways. Lord Lucas made the purchase in his own name, probably in 1912, and held the shooting rights. It is probable that he was responsible for extending and refurbishing the cottage already mentioned, which has since that time been known as Whiteslea Lodge. The three men financed what was to become one of the finest duck shoots in the country, but more importantly they established their estate as a private nature reserve, the second reserve in the country; only Wicken Fen reserve in Cambridgeshire is older, by twelve years.

Opposite page: *E. T. Booth's map of Hickling Broad c 1870, showing the stakes driven into the bed of the broad to mark the channel used by wherries on their way to Hickling Staithe and Catfield. The Hickling keeper's house is marked north of the broad, and "Booth's Boat House" at the south-east corner.*
J. C. Cadbury

A year later Lady Lucas purchased the extensive Horsey estate, to the east of Hickling, which was also declared a nature reserve. Lord Lucas at the same time leased from Colonel Mills the fowling, fishing and sporting rights over part of the estate retained by him for the sum of £255 1s 9d, and thus a very large part of north-east Norfolk was safeguarded against indiscriminate shooting and egg collecting. In 1947 Colonel Mills gave his Hickling estate to his son, Major John Mills and he retains ownership to the present day.

Jim Vincent was employed by Edwin Montagu as head keeper to the Whiteslea estate, with instructions to improve existing habitats for breeding and migrating birds and to develop wildfowl for the shooting season. These tasks became a labour of love for Jim during the next thirty-five years.

Perhaps it was fortunate that a suggestion made in 1913 that Hickling Broad should be taken over as a flying boat base was not taken up, and a naval air station at Great Yarmouth was developed instead. The broad was taken over in 1917 as an emergency landing place for seaplanes and flying boats, and some elderly residents of the village recall that a slipway was constructed near the Pleasure Boat Inn so that aircraft could be dragged out for servicing, but the broad was rarely used in this way.

When Lord Lucas died in 1917 the Whiteslea estate was sold to the Hon. Ivor Grenfell, who retained it until he was killed in a motoring accident in 1926. His father, Lord Desborough (William Henry Grenfell), then took over the estate.

While staying at the Lodge in October, 1927, Lord Desborough got out of bed one morning and stepped into six inches of water. It was not uncommon in those days for the building to flood, for it had been built on boggy marshland only a few inches above

Right: *An old photograph of Hickling taken by Colin Lunn.* Robert Malster

Below: *Whiteslea Lodge, with its lookout against the right-hand wall. It was home to royalty and nobility during the wildfowling season.* S. Linsell

Lord Desborough, seated centre, and his friends at Whiteslea Lodge in 1930. per M. Belson

the normal water level in the broad; the foundations of the wooden walls rested on a bed of faggots. Given a certain combination of new or full moon with severe north-westerly winds there can be a sudden rise of up to two feet in water levels. In 1928 Lord Desborough began a rebuilding programme which included jacking up the original building and providing new, firm foundations beneath that as well as under the new extensions that were added at the same time.

Early in 1944 Lord Desborough decided he could no longer continue visiting his estate at Whiteslea from his home at Taplow in Buckinghamshire, and informed Jim Vincent that he must sell it. Christopher Cadbury, who had been a frequent visitor to Hickling for many years and had come to know Jim Vincent well, was greatly attached to the area. He recalls:

> Jim Vincent wrote to me to tell me that Lord Desborough proposed to sell the Hickling estate, including Whiteslea Lodge. I immediately told him I was interested, and as a result I was offered the estate for £5,000, and I gladly agreed to buy. Sadly, later that year before the negotiations could be completed, both Jim Vincent and Lord Desborough died, without either knowing that the estate was really being bought for the Norfolk Naturalists' Trust.
>
> Lady Gage, who inherited the estate from her father, had to more than double the price to meet estate duties, but in 1946, after the war was ended, the purchase was finally completed in the name of the Norfolk Trust, with contributions from a number of friends.

It is perhaps worth mentioning, in view of the high cost of land today, that the large "island" known as Martham Holmes, bordering the eastern boundary of the Whiteslea estate, came up for sale in 1939. As Christopher Cadbury again recalls:

One day in 1939 Jim Vincent 'phoned me to say that the 300 acres of Martham Holmes was up for sale for £500, but if I held off a little longer he thought he could get it for £300 (£1 per acre). However, in those days I had no permanent connections with Norfolk and was reluctant to take on the responsibilities of this land so far away from my home. Little did I realise at the time quite how important these flood meadows were for birds, especially waders, ducks and swans, being completely surrounded by banks and floodable at will. Soon afterwards war was declared, and this unique and exceptional opportunity was lost for ever.

Fortunately it was not lost for ever. Martham Holmes came up for sale again in 1987 and was purchased by the National Trust.

During the years that he was head keeper to the Whiteslea estate Jim Vincent became well known far beyond Norfolk for the work he did and for his own exceptional qualities. Undoubtedly the highlight of his life was the invitation in 1930 to stay at

The legendary Hickling keeper Jim Vincent calling out the lines of guns for a coot shoot in 1930. His work made the Hickling estate internationally famous as a bird reserve.
per M. Belson

Sandringham for three days as the guest of King George V—an acknowledgement by His Majesty of the happy occasions when he had been wildfowling on Hickling.

In my own modest library of books on natural history there are no fewer than twenty-eight containing references to Hickling and to Jim Vincent. Some idea of the outstanding qualities of the man can be learned from the writings of two of our leading bird photographers, George Yates and Eric Hosking. Writing in *An Eye for a Bird*, the latter tells of a visit to Hickling with his fellow-photographer Cyril Newberry:

> During the period between the two world wars no one visiting Hickling failed sooner or later to meet Jim Vincent . . . he was a lean, lithe man of medium height, strong as a horse, with piercing blue eyes, which could identify an unusual bird at long range without binoculars. He was an expert nest-finder and understood the behaviour of Broadland birds better than anyone else. Jim was the complete Broadsman: he had a good knowledge of boats, was a first-class angler, brilliant shot and an excellent gardener.[7]

George Yates, writing three years after Jim Vincent's death in 1944, describes the necessity of managing reedbeds in a subtle way to provide the specialized habitat required by the bearded tit and tells us:

> The bearded tit seems to be a bird of a specialized habitat within a specialized haunt. Within the reed and sedge beds it is still localized, preferring those with a mat of vegetation over shallow water which has not been cleared for three or four years. It was in appreciation of such subtleties as these that the true greatness of Jim Vincent, the famous Hickling keeper, was revealed. Vincent knew the bearded tit's requirements because he could—or so it seemed—think like a bearded tit. When he "cut" Hickling, he cut in such a way as to leave at all times a number of beds which were in exactly the right state of growth and decay to suit the bearded tit.
>
> To see how true was his knowledge of this little bird's ways it was only necessary to have the privilege of hunting in his company for a nest. In miles and miles of reed and sedge and waterways he would quant his punt to certain particular beds. We would pass many which to my inexperienced eyes looked identical with the one at which we finally stopped. Yet his instinct was sure, and in a good bearded tit year it was odd if there were not birds where he said they would be.[8]

Jim Vincent's son Edwin, writing in that delightful book *A Season of Birds*, tells us this story about his father:

> In my youth at Hickling, it was my good fortune to meet some of the finest ornithologists, bird artists and bird photographers this country has known. They came to meet my father, who had become a legend in his lifetime. I well remember Lord William Percy, who was photographing the bittern on his private estate, Catfield Hall. He brought the first

photographs to show my father, all of which showed only the female bittern at the nest, and said that when he next came he would bring a photograph of male and female on the nest together. My father looked at him quietly, and said: "My Lord, I am not a rich man but I will bet you £5 that you cannot bring me a picture of both birds at the nest." His Lordship, certain of success, replied that he would bet £10 to my father's £5 that he would get the picture; they shook hands on it, and his Lordship left. About two weeks later, he returned to our house, placed two white £5 notes on the table, and asked my father how he was so certain that he would never get the picture. "I will ask your Lordship one question," my father replied. "Did you ever see a cock pheasant on the nest?" His Lordship replied that, of course not, a cock pheasant is polygamous. My father picked up the two fivers, smiled and said, "My Lord, I have proved that the male bittern is polygamous, but it took me twenty years to find it out." His Lordship gracefully acknowledged defeat.[9]

In the summer of 1927 Lord Desborough decided that because of advancing years he must give up the winter shooting on Hickling. On the lawn at Whiteslea Lodge one day he invited a Norfolk sportsman, Colin McLean of Dereham, to form a small syndicate to take over the winter shoot, with Jim Vincent remaining as head keeper. Writing in his book *At Dawn and Dusk*, Colin McLean tells of his enthusiastic response to the suggestion:

> Needless to say I jumped at this, naming Hugh Wormald as one of the guns, and in a few days the syndicate was complete, with Captain Geoffrey Colman and Colonel Oliver Birkbeck as the other two members, who were also most acceptable to Lord Desborough, so the lease was duly fixed up in a very short time.[10]

In his book, which is full of recollections of happy days on Hickling Broad in excellent company, Colin McLean tells one of Jim Vincent's favourite stories:

> Jim was a skilled *raconteur*, and would often regale us after supper in the sitting room at Whiteslea Lodge with tales and amusing anecdotes of the various celebrities who had visited Hickling.
> One of his favourite tales concerned a certain noble lord who, with his valet Thompson, had stayed the night at Whiteslea Lodge after an August evening flight with Lord Desborough. The noble lord had shot very well and had killed over fifty duck to his own gun, and when Jim met his man Thompson after breakfast next morning, he expressed the hope that his lordship had enjoyed his evening flight. "By gum," replied Thompson, "he must have done, for he put on his braces *himself* this morning, and that's the first time he's ever done that since I've been with him!"[11]

Jim Vincent's days as keeper at Hickling came to an end in 1944 when he became seriously ill. He died on 4th November, 1944, and many were the tributes paid to his work in protecting and conserving rare birds during his thirty-five years as head keeper. Let a tribute in the local newspaper from Dr B. B. Riviere, author of *A History of the Birds of Norfolk*, stand for them all:

> As headkeeper on the Hickling estate he was given by Lord Desborough an almost free hand in its management. Birds were his passion, and he devoted all his energies to making it a reserve. Long experience and unequalled knowledge of the habits of ducks, waders, bitterns and harriers enabled him by a planned system of flooding, draining, grazing and cutting to enhance and maintain its attractiveness until it has become today world famous, and a sort of Mecca for birdlovers from far and near. It is largely due to him that the marsh harriers, Montagu's harriers and bitterns, all of which had become extinct, have returned to the county as breeding species, and that that rare, delightful and essentially Norfolk little bird, the bearded tit, has been able to maintain its precarious status . . .
>
> To wildfowlers and shooting men he was equally well known. He was a first-class shot at geese, duck or game, and as a fisherman could prove on occasion as deadly to the Wye salmon as to his native Hickling pike . . .
>
> Hickling can never be quite the same without him, and the birds have lost their best friend.[12]

Let the last word about this legendary keeper come from his sister, Ida Grosvenor, who lived in nearby Ludham until her death

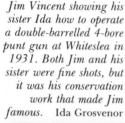

Jim Vincent showing his sister Ida how to operate a double-barrelled 4-bore punt gun at Whiteslea in 1931. Both Jim and his sister were fine shots, but it was his conservation work that made Jim famous. Ida Grosvenor

in her ninety-eighth year. The tales she had to tell about the old days at Hickling were legion, and she has her own place in local history, for there was a time when her name was as well known as her brother's. Among the many stories Ida told me about her brother this is the one I like best:

My brother Jim used to get up to a lot of mischief, particularly with some of the important visitors who came to Whiteslea for the shooting. Some of these Lords and Sirs he couldn't get on with, as they didn't do what he told them when they went shooting. Jim had a favourite trick how to get his own back on them. Sometimes they would stay for the evening flight until it was too dark to see anything, and this would mean crossing a ligger (plank) over a dyke to reach their punt. Perhaps one of these Lordships, whom Jim didn't like, would reach a ligger and say he couldn't see it. He had a job to know where to put his feet. So, Jim, who had already crossed, would stand in the middle of it facing his Lordship. He then struck several matches to show the way over. His Lordship slowly walked the ligger when Jim would light no more matches, saying he was sorry but he hadn't got any more. Of course, the light from the matches had blinded his Lordship, who now didn't know where to put his feet. The next thing that happened was his Lordship fell off the ligger into the dyke, and crawled out smelling something terrible!

Ida has her own place in the local scene, for she could sail a

Ida Vincent shooting beside Deep Dyke in 1931, doubtless to the consternation of the passing yachtsmen. She was only five when she borrowed her father's gun to shoot a pigeon, and in 1936 she represented Britain in the Olympic Games in Berlin.
Ida Grosvenor

boat and quant a punt with the best of men; she was determined from an early age to make her own way in a male-dominated world. She was only five when she took her father's walking-stick gun when he was not about, carried it into the garden, took aim at a pigeon perched on a chimneypot, fired and shot it dead. Then at the age of twelve she crept out of the house with her father's 12-bore, and returned home with her first two wild ducks.

From then on there was no stopping her. Ultimately she became one of the finest shots in Britain, representing England in the DTL International Championships in 1927, 1932 and 1934; to this day she is the only woman to have represented England in this event. In 1936 she shot for Britain at the Olympic Games in Berlin.

Among her proudest possessions were the Purdey "Special" cartridges stamped with a crown which were used by King George VI when out shooting at Hickling.

Following Jim Vincent's death Ted Piggin, who had been underkeeper for a number of years, became the estate keeper and warden. He held the post until shortly before his death in 1965. During those twenty years he and Christopher Cadbury began a series of tasks for the improvement of the reserve which were aimed both at conserving existing flora and fauna and at attracting new species, as well as providing facilities for visitors. A sluice system was introduced by which water levels on marshes and wader pools could be raised and lowered as required. Bird-hides were put up at Rush Hills, Swim Coots and Deary's, and considerable excavations were carried out at Swim Coots.

One who was employed in these tasks was George Bishop, of Hickling. Born on 26th July, 1902, George spent his early working years on a local fruit farm and with a building firm at Catfield, then joined Ted Piggin on the Whiteslea estate in 1939. His wife Margaret, tells me he particularly enjoyed punting nobility on the annual coot shoots, as well as taking part in the making of the film *Conflict of Wings*, when he led an armada of irate villagers across the broad to thwart the bombing of an island. Although George Bishop retired in 1965 he returned as warden following Ted Piggin's death, but died himself in 1970.

His successor as warden was Lieutenant-Colonel Bob Sankey, recently retired from the Royal Marines after a distinguished career that saw him decorated with the DSO and DSC. It was he who carried out instructions to have Whiteslea Lodge quay-headed all round to prevent it being flooded in winter by high water in the broad. He also founded the unique and very popular water trail, which gained a special Duke of Edinburgh Countryside Award in 1970. He was responsible for the construction of the thatch and glass observation hut on the Whiteslea wall overlooking the broad and for the new wader pools which he made on the nearby marsh,

Opposite page: Ted Piggin, who took over as estate keeper and warden on Jim Vincent's death in 1944. With Christopher Cadbury he was reponsible for many improvements aimed at attracting new species and providing better facilities for visitors.

Lieutenant-Colonel Bob Sankey with an injured osprey. Bob Sankey was warden from 1968 to 1974 and was responsible for founding the highly successful water trail.
Dr K. J. Carlson

and he was also responsible for the building of the tree tower in Whiteslea Wood. Sadly, he was taken ill in 1974 and died on 18th April, 1975.

Arthur Beales, who had worked on the reserve since leaving the Royal Navy in 1947, acted as reserve warden while Bob Sankey was ill and kept the water trail operating, as well as superintending the other two boat tours and the walking trail. During the time he worked on the reserve he accumulated a great fund of knowledge about the reserve and its inhabitants, and nobody was more aware than he of the dramatic changes that had taken place in the waterways and the reed- and sedgebeds. Who could have been better qualified than he to fill the vacancy until a new warden was appointed?

I was that new warden. After leaving the Essex Naturalists' Trust nature reserve at Fingringhoe Wick I took up my duties on 26th May, 1975, and it was to Arthur that I went when I wanted to know about the reserve. I am indebted to him for much of the information in this book about the old Whiteslea estate and the present reserve, which he always kept in such good shape. Visitors often expressed their praise to me at the way the pathways were kept, making them such a joy to walk, and at the way he looked after the wader pools, which in a good growing summer had to be mown three times in order to attract migrating wading birds and others, and to enable visitors in the bird-hides to see them.

In February, 1969, Norman Belson of Hickling, who had previously spent nearly twenty years working on local farms, including Waxham Hall, was employed to assist Arthur Beales in the management of the reserve. Their partnership proved to be an excellent and friendly one. Then in August, 1974, George Taylor of Potter Heigham joined the staff on leaving school. George remained on the Hickling staff until in 1986 he was appointed warden of Broadland reserves owned by the Norfolk Naturalists' Trust. His place was ultimately filled at Hickling by David Jenkin of Ingham.

Arthur Beales had been on the reserve for forty-one years when he retired at the end of October, 1988. Rob Scott was appointed to fill the resulting vacancy.

Many people over the years have rendered great service in assisting with management tasks, for there is a great deal to be done on a reserve which is visited by some six thousand people every year. All of them earn the heartfelt thanks of the warden, who at times can be hard pressed. Volunteers have helped with the running of the water trail and other boat tours, with escorting parties on the walking trails, manning the office, helping to control vermin, policing the reserve, clearing up the prodigious amount of litter left on those banks where holiday boats are moored, collecting fishing dues and all kinds of other jobs.

Local people can do a great deal to help the warden of a reserve such as Hickling. Billy Nudd, who gave me his account of the 1938 flood, is still very active in spite of his eighty-two years and is the proverbial fount of all knowledge about Hickling's past as well as its present. He has been in charge of the parish staithe and moorings for very many years, and anyone wanting to know where they can moor, keep or launch a boat simply has to ask Billy.

Another local character well known to generations of holiday-makers, especially those who arrived by boat, was Waldo Beales, who died in 1985 at the age of eighty-eight. For many decades he had run his small boatyard and garage at the staithe behind the Pleasure Boat Inn, and it was there that I first met him in the Easter holidays in 1939, when our headmaster and a group of boys from Bishop's Stortford College hired Waldo's three half-deckers, *Marigold*, *Marguerite* and *Meadowsweet*; we learned to sail in them.

There were undoubtedly characters among the local people

Left: *This photograph of the Pleasure Boat Inn, Hickling, was taken by Payne Jennings in 1877. The building had been enlarged by the time Miss Emma Turner used it as her supply base.*
per Gwen Amis

Below: *Miss Emma Turner in her houseboat* Water Rail *in 1922, making friends with one of the mute swans then inhabiting the broad.*
per Julia Turner

and those employed on the reserve, and there were certainly characters among those who have visited the estate over the years. Without doubt the best-known woman on the Hickling scene was Miss Emma Turner, one of our pioneer bird photographers; it was she who with Jim Vincent found the bittern had returned to breed in Norfolk at nearby Sutton Broad in 1911. A frequent visitor to Hickling in the early years of this century, she had a wooden hut constructed on an island in the broad which she used regularly, winter and summer, for twenty years. She kept a houseboat called the *Water-Rail* permanently moored there, and to get about the broad she had a canoe, *Ezekiel*, a flat-bottomed rowing boat, the *Merrythought*, and a sailing dinghy, *Bittern*. Some of Miss Turner's remarkable photographs were published in *Broadland Birds*, one of her many books, in 1924. Today it is keenly sought on the second-hand market by book collectors.

I recall coming back up the broad at the conclusion of one of our Water Trails in 1976 and telling my visitors, as usual when passing Turner's Island, about this remarkable woman. A man sitting in the boat asked me what on earth she did for drinking

Miss Turner's Island at Hickling Broad in 1985. The name recalls the period when Miss Turner had a wooden hut on the island which she used summer and winter alike when photographing birds at Hickling.   S. Linsell

water—"surely she didn't have to fetch it from the Pleasure Boat Inn every time she wanted some?" he remarked. When I replied that I had no idea a young woman sitting on the front seat spoke up. "I can answer that question for you! I'm Julia Turner, and you've been talking about my great-aunt. We've always understood in our family that she drank water out of the broad." In those days, of course, that water was crystal clear.

Gwen Amis, who in those days lived at the Pleasure Boat Inn with her parents, tells me that she remembers her father setting off in his boat, winter and summer alike, with provisions, newspapers and mail for Miss Turner. And if Alfred Amis was unable to go, Gwen would either row or quant the boat to Turner's Island with the supplies.

When Emma Turner died in 1940 many national newspapers as well as ornithological journals carried her obituary. *The Ibis*, the long-established journal of the British Ornithologists' Union,

Roland Green shows off the friezes which he painted for Whiteslea Lodge in 1930. Among the group are Miss Emma Turner, third from left, and Dr B. B. Riviere, author of A History of the Birds of Norfolk.
Norfolk Naturalists' Trust

referred to her as "a woman pioneer who occupied a foremost place in the ranks of ornithologists" and went on:

> Though frequently alone in her houseboat on Hickling Broad, she never felt the loneliness ascribed to her by the Press. Her joy in Nature by day and night was too vivid to admit of loneliness! Several honours came to Miss Turner on account of her admirable work in the furtherance of ornithology. She was one of the first of the small band of women to be admitted as Fellows of the Linnean Society. She was also among the first woman members of the British Ornithologists' Union.

Another well-known figure at Hickling was the famous bird artist Roland Green, who lived beside the broad near Hill Common. In 1930 he was commissioned by Lord Desborough to paint four huge friezes for the sitting room of Whiteslea Lodge. They occupy the whole length and breadth of the four walls and depict the views from the lookout to the north, south, east and west; the two largest were 26 feet long, the other two 17 feet in length. These remarkable friezes contain pictures of the birds that were typical of the area at the time.

A highlight in the history of the country's second oldest nature reserve came in 1976, when the Norfolk Naturalists' Trust celebrated its golden jubilee. In the summer of that year the Hickling reserve was visited by officers from most of the other county trusts, who saw demonstrations of our various machines on a beautifully sunny day; the swallowtails put on a great show, to everyone's delight.

An important part of the jubilee celebrations was the opening of a conservation centre at the edge of Ranworth Broad by the Queen and Prince Philip. During the ceremony my wife and I, the Hickling staff and the wardens from the other Trust reserves were presented to Her Majesty and His Royal Highness.

During the twelve and a half years that I was warden at Hickling we had a substantial increase in the number of visitors enjoying the self-guided trails and the water tours. School parties came not only from Norfolk but from Nottinghamshire, Leicestershire, Suffolk, Essex and Hertfordshire, and we were able to welcome visitors, too, from many foreign countries, notably Holland, France, Germany, the Scandinavian countries and the United States of America, and also from China and Japan.

With increasing numbers of people coming to the reserve it was necessary to improve facilities for visitors; a new two-and-a-half-mile nature trail was laid out, and additional bird-hides were put up overlooking the wader pools. Some of the existing hides were enlarged, and new wader pools were excavated and old ones enlarged.

It was Herbert Axell, the RSPB Senior Warden, who introduced me to the management of wader pools many years ago. He had pioneered wetland habitat development at Minsmere on the Suffolk coast between 1959 and 1975, and he deserves not only my thanks but the thanks of all conservationists for passing on the results of his experience. On his annual visits to Hickling with his wife Joan, and usually with other conservationists from Britain and overseas, he was always kind enough to express pleasure at the variety of birds present on the various pools.

A never-ending task is keeping the water levels in the wader pools always right, whatever the time of year, and keeping the shingle islands free of vegetation in order to attract nesting species like the ringed plover, oystercatcher, lapwing and tern. The vital requirements are to keep water levels high over winter to benefit the invertebrates on which the birds feed, to help control plant growth and to attract waterfowl. Between early spring and autumn lower water levels are required to give areas of mud as well as an expanse of shallow water. When the young birds have fledged comes the time to mow invading vegetation that would if not controlled take over the pool. It is most important never to let the exposed mud dry out completely; there should always be enough

Alastair McLean, president of the Norfolk Naturalists' Trust, introducing Nature Conservancy Council chairman Sir William Wilkinson at the opening of a new public bird-hide at Hickling. S. Linsell

water in the pool to keep it moist, except where anaerobic conditions have developed and drying out is necessary to promote reoxygenation.

There is always so much to do on a reserve. Management demands a great deal of attention and effort, but it is something that brings its rewards.

My time as warden came to an end on 31st October, 1987. With my retirement Francis Russell was appointed warden and took up his duties the day after I finished. For him the work was just beginning.

"Beavers", members of the Broads Authority's conservation group, constructing shingle islands on Rush Hills.
S. Linsell

Royal Occasions 3

ENTRIES in the Whiteslea Lodge game books, which record all shoots on Hickling Broad between 1911 and 1961, contain the names of dukes, earls and other members of the nobility, of two Prime Ministers, and of many famous people who have enjoyed the shooting on the estate. Even two Kings and other members of the Royal Family have been to Hickling to take part in shoots.

King George VI enjoyed many wildfowling days in Norfolk, not only on the Royal Estate at Sandringham but at Holkham on the North Norfolk coast and on the Broads at Hickling and Ranworth. A keen wildfowler, he spent many a cold but pleasant hour out on the broad in a punt or ensconced in a reed and timber butt among the reeds.

His father, King George V, visited Hickling on only two occasions during his reign, when he came for a day's wildfowling on the broad as a guest of Lord Desborough. Both times he was driven to Whiteslea from Sandringham, where he and his family customarily spent the Christmas and New Year holiday.

However, King George V was never such a keen wildfowler as his son, who as Duke of York and later as King George VI visited Hickling on any number of occasions. Many of those carefree days are recorded by Aubrey Buxton in *The King in his Country*. I quote first from Lord Buxton's account of a visit to Hickling in 1938:

> The King and his companions arrived at Woodbastwick for luncheon on January 2nd and a three-day plan was evolved in eager consultation. Outside the wintry scene proclaimed with grim assurance that a cold spell had come to stay. However, intermittent snow showers made the party hopeful that the weather would remain rough without too much frost, and at all costs it was hoped that the open Broads would not become frozen over. Soon the car was out once more on the deserted by-roads on the way to Hickling. The maroon Daimler, speckled with frozen snowflakes, moved silently over the last stretch of the snow-carpeted drive to the shooting lodge.
>
> In summer, sedge and reed-warblers chatter a staccato chorus in the dykes alongside, grasshopper warblers reel in the thick marsh grass, and harriers beat lazily about their territories on either side. The strange booming of the bittern, the "bitterbum" or "bogbumper" of an earlier age, punctuates the stillness like a phantom double bass.
>
> But to-day it was a harsh spectacle, the dykes lifeless and solid with ice, reeds and long grass frosted and fast. No birds spoke in the bleak afternoon on the marshland, and only the duck shooters' accustomed

Opposite page: *King George VI with Aubrey Buxton at Whiteslea Lodge after a coot shoot on Hickling Broad on 27th January, 1951. It was a perfect day, Aubrey Buxton later wrote; it was also the King's last visit to Hickling.*
J. C. Cadbury

Assembling at the Pleasure Boat Inn for a coot shoot in February, 1930. per M. Belson

abundance of optimism would have explained to the unversed the merry countenances of the company which fore-gathered for tea at the lodge.

This white, reed-thatched bungalow stands on an island lawn amongst the reed-beds, surrounded by dykes and channels which lead out to the open water and to the Broad proper. The ice was thick and

snow-covered in the channels, and in the normal event the lodge would have been sealed off altogether and no movement from it afloat would have been possible. However, Jim Vincent, the head keeper, and his men, in expectation of a visit by His Majesty, had worked continuously and hard in their punts and succeeded in keeping a passageway clear of ice. . .

Vincent quanted the King through the passage, breaking as they progressed a thin skin of ice which was already forming again on the surface. As they neared Swimcotes, a stream of coots flew back over the punt and the King had a merry "battue" from his seat, killing thirty, which mostly fell on the ice and were retrieved later by the dogs. His Majesty occupied a dry sheltered tub by the side of the slad, and settled in to wait for the flight.

That evening they enjoyed a sporting flight. But the sky was dark and a light snow fell spasmodically. The duck came early, which was as well since because of the heavy cloud and early darkness it was not long before they were all picking up. The King shot over forty tufted duck and pochard, an exhilarating experience while it lasted. He got as well a handful of mallard and one goldeneye . . . It was very dark when the King left Swimcotes with Vincent, and falling snow reduced visibility to nil. To be out in the total exposure of East Norfolk within two miles of the North Sea on such a night would not be to everyone's taste, but for the King, his punt carrying a cargo of plump diving ducks, it was enthralling.

Snow fell heavily during the night, and Colin McLean had a rough trip next day from Dereham. Nevertheless he and Percy and Meredith Perrin were assembled at the lodge at nine o'clock.

They waited for some time with no news of the King, until finally at ten-thirty a message was brought by a policeman to say that the royal car had been snowed up on the way, and had been forced to turn back.

This was the end of the King's Broadland visit on that occasion. After the high expectations with which he set forth, it must have been something of a disappointment that the schedule was in the end cut to two evening flights.[1]

The highlight and finale of the shooting season on Hickling was always the coot shoots, which His Majesty attended on several occasions. Although wildfowlers had shot coot for the pot for a very long time, it was Lord Desborough who introduced specific shoots as a conservation measure earlier in this century. There is no small measure of irony concerning this, in view of what has happened in recent times. Lord Desborough realized that unless he took steps to cull the huge wintering coot population, which varied in number between 2,000 and 4,000 according to Jim Vincent's diaries, the aquatic flora in the broad would be drastically reduced. Over the past three decades we humans with our pollutants and dredging activities have done a much better job of destroying the water plants than the coots ever did.

No history of Hickling Broad would be complete without

relating how those coot shoots were carried out. Who better to tell us than Colin McLean:

The job of driving the coot is not easy, especially when there are not sufficient punts out. The punts fan out in line with both flanks slightly in advance, and moving along quite slowly drive all the coot ahead to the north end of the Broad in the vicinity of the Pleasure Boat Inn, where it narrows considerably; while this operation is in progress a number of the coot may decide that they have moved down far enough, and start to break back; then, if the boats are not evenly spaced, they judge the distance very cleverly and all break over any gap.

As the punts near the end they halt, and one is sent on ahead round the shore to flush the coot which come back over the guns at varying heights. Jim Vincent, as commodore of the fleet, usually was in the centre, using a megaphone to keep the line in order, and woe betide the quanter who got too far ahead or who lagged behind! At this drive all the shooting is done from boats in a sitting position, and birds passing on one's right are not easy; it really pays to concentrate on those coming straight overhead or on one's left front, and even then, to one who has not tried the game before, they are difficult. They certainly fly high, sometimes almost out of shot, but if coming upwind they do not appear to be moving at any speed; actually they are sideslipping nearly all the time, and are much easier when flying fast straight downwind. Two boats follow behind the line to pick up, and on reaching the north end of the Broad, the punts re-form in line with the right well ahead and push those that have settled again through a narrow channel by Miss Turner's island into Heigham Corner.

For the second drive some of the guns go ashore on each side of the channel, and four or five are left in wooden butts built above water-level across the entrance. A couple of gunning punts then go round and flush the coot, driving them back over the guns.

Sometimes when the wind is favourable the coot are driven back to the main Broad over the Swimcotes slad; when this is possible they generally fly very high, and after they have been over the guns a couple of times they certainly learn to seek safety by flying high or by slipping out sideways if they get half a chance. Once the leaf is off the reeds, they never seem to want to take refuge in the dense reed-beds at the edge of the Broad, and tend more and more to bunch together in the open.

It is usually possible to get in five or six drives in a day, but if there is a high wind picking-up takes longer and four drives is enough. On getting back to Whiteslea Lodge the coot are laid out in rows of fifty, but in the days before Lord Desborough made the road to Whiteslea Lodge we used to finish up at the Pleasure Boat Inn, and all the villagers assembled on the staithe to have their two brace of coot each.[2]

It is staggering to learn that between December, 1894, and February, 1935, a total of 33,546 coot were shot on Hickling Broad. And between 1920 and 1947 a total of 23,788 assorted duck were shot, which included sixty-six garganey. Small wonder there is so much lead shot in the silt on the bottom of the broad!

King George VI last visited Whiteslea Lodge and Hickling Broad in January, 1951, when he attended a coot shoot. As Aubrey Buxton relates:

The scene during the drive presented a dramatic and unforgettable picture. After a violent squall of sleet and hail the storm had blown eastwards and shafts of sunlight pierced the scurrying cloud-masses and defined sunlit areas of striking beauty amidst the darkened landscape. Reed-beds were a shimmering russet and gold, as if a fire glowed within them, whereas in heavy shadow they were sepia. The restless waters, in shadow a leaden grey, suddenly sparkled in the

A coot shoot under way on the broad on 7th February, 1930. No fewer than 843 coot were shot. per M. Belson

sunlight into the deepest royal-blue, flecked with dancing silver. Every bird, from swan to teal, seemed to be catapulted across a sky of rich deep colours and undisguised fury. The coots, ingeniously driven across the gale, filled the sky like wind-tossed leaves over the centre butts.

And once again, to lend a vivid touch to a Norfolk landscape, in the centre of this bold canvas was His Majesty the King in a reed and timber butt which stands on four stilts out in the Broad; and a King, in a classical wildfowl setting to which he truly belonged, as content as anything in this world could make him. Over a hundred coots were picked up in the vicinity of his butt, shots which ranged from low scuttlers to inspiring downwind gallery shots and crossers well out to a flank. Boatmen and some of the guns were content to stand and watch. If a handful of incidents were to be selected as exceptional moments in the life of a shooting sovereign, this would certainly have been one of them.

In the following year entirely different conditions awaited the King. If it is possible to conceive the exact opposite of that stormy day, this was it. The day was so warm that many of the pushers removed their jackets. The sunshine was so generous that it might have been September or October. And even the most venerable and experienced of ancient coot shooters present could not remember the surface of the Broad being so totally calm in January. There was literally not one tremor, nor a tremble, over all those three hundred acres, and the reflections of the reeds and the birds, of men and punts, were clear and beautiful in the limpid waters.

It was the happiest of days, with the happiest of company. There were gathered together not only some of His Majesty's lifelong friends, and especially companions of fen and broad, but also a truly representative team of the Norfolk shooting fraternity. Once more, as had happened at Sandringham on a morning flight, this might have been a set-piece, the whole scene and the arrangement grouped around the person of the wildfowler King, with wonderful weather to enhance the charm and the magic of Broadland. This was a perfect day and, looking back, how splendid that it was so.

For, as it proved, this was His Majesty's last day in Broadland.

As he stepped from his punt in the afternoon sunshine, after a day of cheerful companionship and vigorous sport, he stepped from a Norfolk punt for the last time. This great sportsman, our King, whose flight-shooting in East Norfolk will become legendary, was making his last round. For in the twenty-four hours beforehand he had been on Ranworth Flood and Cockshoot. Now, for a final day in Broadland company, he was at Hickling.

As his car bore him away along the marshland drive, the King of England saw for the last time reed-beds glowing in the sunset and the horizon mirrored in still waters.

In the nineteen-fifties and up to January, 1961, the Duke of Edinburgh, a great conservationist as well as wildfowler, was a fairly regular visitor to Hickling and to Whiteslea Lodge. On two occasions he brought his son, Prince Charles, later Prince of Wales, with him. One of those visits is proudly remembered by Gwen Amis, landlady of the Pleasure Boat Inn at Hickling staithe at the time. It was the weekend of 9th–11th January, 1959.

A week previously Major Aubrey Buxton, organiser of the shoot, had noted at Whiteslea Lodge the abnormally high water in the broad, and feared that with the water likely to rise still higher it would be out of the question to accommodate the Royal guests there the next weekend. Accordingly he made provisional arrangements with Mr and Mrs Amis for the shooting party to be put up at the inn. By the weekend there was a foot of water inside the lodge.

At about 4.30 pm on the Friday Albert and Gwen Amis were at home having a cup of tea. Major Buxton and Ted Piggin the keeper were out on reconnaissance and concluded that the conditions were impossible for shooting next day. The Duke and the Prince were not expected until later, but, as Gwen well recalls:

> Suddenly the door to our kitchen opened and there stood the Duke of Edinburgh, and behind him was the Prince of Wales and Lord Brabourne. I asked them to come in, and I soon made them some fresh tea.
>
> Everything was ready for the Royal guests. Electric heaters were already on and a fire was burning in my private lounge, which was placed at the Duke's disposal. We had only three rooms for visitors at

King George VI and the Right Hon. David Bowes Lyon setting off from Whiteslea Lodge on 11th February, 1950.
per M. Belson

the inn. The Duke occupied one bedroom and the Prince slept in another with two other little boys. One was Lord Brabourne's son and the other was Timothy Buxton. The three boys occupied separate beds in the same room. I did all the catering. We had no waiters, cooks or anything like that. Dinner was served in the dining room, with the three boys eating first, and the Duke and his guest later. I laid on a normal meal, nothing special, and they all said how good it was.

On the Saturday morning Prince Philip insisted on going out, but it was snowing and bitterly cold. The party returned for lunch, but Prince Charles did not go out again in the afternoon. Instead, he and the other two boys watched television and saw Norwich beat Manchester.

That evening, being Saturday, the inn was full of locals, whilst the Royal guests were upstairs. There was a hell of a noise going on overhead, a lot of yelling and shouting and thumpings on the floor. Some of the lads at the bar reckoned I had got a load of rats upstairs. After a while I went up and told the boys to be quiet, and as I turned to leave the room the Duke stood behind me. "That's right, Mrs Amis", he said, "you tell them to behave." He picked up a rolled umbrella, handed it to me, and suggested I lay it across them. I didn't, of course, but they were less noisy. Those boys had been having a good old pillow-fight.

Gwen never revealed to anyone which beds the Duke and the Prince slept in; nor does anybody, other than herself, know what the Royal guests were given to eat that weekend, and on other visits. But she has kindly allowed me to extract from her scrapbook the bill she presented to Major Buxton covering the accommodation and all meals for five persons for the weekend of 2nd and 3rd January, plus six persons with full board for the following weekend, and meals for one detective and one chauffeur; the total cost was £32.

It was in January, 1961, that Prince Philip last visited the shooting lodge at Whiteslea for a weekend's duck and coot shooting on the broad. He was among the last sportsmen to do so, for all shooting ceased on the broad and Heigham Sounds at the beginning of February.

The final entry in the game book is reproduced on the opposite page.

The Duke of Edinburgh and Prince Charles setting out from Whiteslea, with Ted Piggin quanting, in January, 1958.
per M. Belson

Through the Seasons 4 at Hickling

MANY PEOPLE see the Broads in summer and autumn, when the waterways are alive with boats of every description. Certainly the area has a charm of its own in every season, and many are captivated by that charm, but those who know the rivers and broads only in the holiday season do not really know them at all.

Late autumn is a most rewarding time on Hickling, especially when the sun shines and the miles of reedbeds glow like ripe corn. Gone are the boats, except for a few "locals", and gone too are the blaring cassette-radios. There is a tremendous peace beneath this vast umbrella of sky, a peace broken only by the call of a wild duck or some marsh bird. This is a place and a season of superbly colourful sunrises and sunsets, especially the latter. To stand on the lookout at Whiteslea at the going down of a blood-red sun which turns the whole western sky aflame, as tens of thousands of gulls and millions of starlings assemble to roost, is a privilege accorded to few people. Most things around the world are changing, not for the better, but the splendour of Hickling on a clear autumn evening will never change.

It does sometimes happen that on an evening or two in October or November the wind, which seems to blow the whole year round, fritters away to a whisper and the waterways are completely still. Not a ripple disturbs the surface and there is a rare peaceful calm. This is the time to get a punt out and quietly push oneself wherever the mood takes one. There was such an evening in late October, 1977. I drove to Whiteslea. The sun had set some time before, but there was still a deep blush in the western sky. I looked eastwards and saw a full moon climbing above the horizon. I could hear the murmured voices of fishermen a long way down Heigham Sounds. From the broad and the reedbeds around it came the massive yet subdued murmurings of hordes of starlings and gulls.

I just wished I could see one of the local barn owls gliding on silent wings over the reed tops and stretching a leg down to grab a starling as it dozed off. For this is what the owls have learned to do. There cannot be an easier way to get a meal. Having plucked their victim off a reed stem they fly with it to the steps of our bird-hides,

Opposite page: *George Bishop feeding wildfowl on Hickling Broad on 12th January, 1968. The ducks take full advantage of the handout, the mute swans and geese remain just out of reach, and the coots for the most part stand off in the background.*
Mrs M. Bishop

69

where they do a neat dismembering job. Next morning I may find up to three sets of wings and heads at one hide, for this is all they leave after their moments of surgery.

From nearby came the regular calls of a coypu, a strange, haunting, lamb-like bleating sound. I just wished I might hear the whistle of an otter, but this is one animal I neither saw nor heard at Hickling. The coypu trappers have occasionally come across the remains of a roach or a bream which they reckoned had been eaten by an otter, and a local farmer was positive he heard one whistling near Meadow Dyke during darkness in the late nineteen-seventies. I did once have the rare sight of a family of otters at play under a full moon in Norfolk, but that was not at Hickling.

This was a night to drift silently over the water, giving an occasional push with the quant to keep steerage way on. Only some mallard appeared annoyed by my presence; they rose with noisy wings and cries of alarm, shattering the stillness. Coypu continued bleating, a pochard "purred" quietly across what is left of Whiteslea Broad, a water rail squealed nearby and in the distance a tawny owl called. I glided down Deep-Go-Dyke with the last light in the western sky almost gone, and everywhere bathed in moonlight. A solitary sailing cruiser was moored against the quay-heading, its crew oblivious to my passing.

And then comes winter. Oak, birch and alder stand gaunt and naked, gales and frosts having stripped their branches of foliage, once green and then bronzed. The same agencies have left the reeds bereft of their golden leaves, and their thin stems with purple feathery plumes bend to the winds.

Above all, there is now a wonderful peace. Sometimes in the depth of winter I stand on the lookout at Whiteslea, or on the tree tower in the nearby wood, and revel in the silence and the beauty of the scenery.

There was a time, of course, when a few people could be seen in winter, and not so very long ago at that. There were the ardent wildfowlers and the hardy pike-fishermen, for whom the cold aloofness of winter held a peculiar charm. And hidden away in the remoteness of the reedbeds were the equally hardy breed of Norfolk marshmen, busily harvesting the reeds. They continue their trade today, but it is unlikely that the visitor to Broadland at this time of year will see anything of them. Nowadays the sight of a winter fisherman on Hickling Broad or Heigham Sounds is a fairly rare one; the toxic alga *Prymnesium* has wrought havoc with the fish populations.

Winter has its own magic for those who are around. The bitter winds rattle the dry stems of the reeds, and cold mists enshroud the

Cadbury's Pool in the grip of winter. S. Linsell

marshes; in such conditions one can soon be chilled to the marrow. Yet it needs no more than a gleam of sunshine to rekindle the fire in the reedbeds and to set the marshes aglow once again. Even when stinging rain falls relentlessly all day, the marsh vegetation takes on a wonderful colour, for as it becomes more and more sodden it changes from grey to brown, and from brown to reddish purple. And when the rain stops silence seems to brood over the marshes and waterways. At times even the ubiquitous wildfowl are silenced by the pageantry of a winter's dawn, when the air is stilled and marshes rimed by a hoar frost.

Prolonged spells of Arctic weather normally see most of the waterways frozen hard, but the few wildfowl that remain in the area manage to keep open a small patch of water somewhere or other. The icing process will be delayed on the broad and the Sounds if strong winds accompany the first few nights of hard frost, for then the wave action is sufficient to keep the water open. There is one thing I have noted at Hickling: no matter what the season is, gales very rarely last more than three days.

In January and February, 1985, it was possible to walk or skate from the Pleasure Boat Inn over most of the broad. Some enterprising people fitted skids to sailing dinghies and sailed across the ice. I took a brace and bit and a steel tape-measure, and found the ice was up to six inches thick in places. Arthur Beales tells me that in the bitter winter of 1963 the ice on the broad was fourteen inches thick, and locals ran their cars on to it and skated by the light of head lamps after dark.

In 1985 it was mostly coot and mallard that kept open three small areas of water, appreciated by a few other wildfowl including several smew and goosanders. Sheltered dykes and ditches in woods and spinneys are afforded protection against any but the most severe night frosts, and these oases enable secretive and retiring birds like the water rail and woodcock to survive; and they provide drinking water for blackbirds, song thrushes, fieldfares, redwing and the small passerines.

On the few occasions when I have seen the broad frozen over I have witnessed a very odd sight: ruffs, two or three dozen of them, walking over the ice and feeding when a thaw occurs during the day; I can only assume that as the surface ice melts certain invertebrates are released from an icy tomb, and it is these that the ruffs are feeding on. No other waders have been observed doing this.

In such weather I once saw a greater black-backed gull fly up from a patch of ice-free water with a luckless coot, which was carried for some fifty feet before being dropped on to the ice. It was then seized again, and dropped on to the ice; after this had been repeated four times the coot ceased to try to evade the gull, which began feeding on it.

I have seen something of this kind on only one other occasion. That was many years ago at Abberton reservoir in Essex, when a greater black-backed gull seized a sickly or "pricked" teal from a patch of clear water. Although the victim sought desperately to evade the gull's attack by diving, each time it surfaced the gull was after it.

Why the gulls did not carry their victims on to the ice and simply kill them I shall never know.

Spells of arctic weather in nearly all my winters at Hickling brought in exciting visitors from the north: whooper and Bewick's swans, whitefronts, pinkfeet and barnacle geese, and on rare occasions small parties of snow buntings.

There is nothing quite so thrilling as the calls of wild swans. Their cries are first heard a long way off, and nearer and nearer comes the baying sound; then they are visible high above, as they come down the wind in wedge formation, their bodies almost as dazzling as the snowfields they have left. It is one of Nature's great sights.

Frequently wild swans fly into the broad as the last light of day pales to darkness, and there they remain throughout the night. No matter what time I put my head out of doors or open the bedroom window, I hear them talking away among themselves. On a still night the tenor calls of the Bewick's mingle with the baritone voices of the whoopers to produce a wonderful muted chorus. Sometimes they favour Horsey Mere for their nightly roost; if the light wind is easterly their murmurings still reach me one and a half miles away.

As February slips away there are signs that another bitter winter will, hopefully, soon be gone. The days are lengthening, of course, and four vocalists welcome this: song thrush, robin, yellowhammer and chaffinch. The great tit on mild days adds its spring-time *"teacher-teacher"* calls. Towards the end of the month, on fine still days, other calls can be heard from the wader pools as the first resident birds return from their winter wanderings: lapwing, ringed plover and redshank. So often this foretaste of spring may be succeeded by bitter winds, frost and snow, but those few warm days have done their work. Nature has not merely stretched and yawned: she is awake, and the spring urge grows daily in intensity.

The transition from winter to spring at Hickling is quite unpredictable, but then I suppose this can be said of any place in Britain. There are some who will tell you that "we don't get springs no nore", and there is a fair bit of truth in this. The pattern seems to have evolved over the last two decades that although March is wintry it often produces a spell of warm sunny days; April is often wet and raw cold, but can also come up with a few real spring-like days; then winter bites once more and the weather remains cold for much of May, as many a holidaymaker on his cruiser has discovered.

One is aware of every day-to-day change in this wide, open and bleak corner of Norfolk, especially if one's work is out of doors virtually every day of the week. It seems to be an annual feature these past many years for the winds to get away from the west, where they have remained nearly all winter, and into the north-east about the middle of April. And there they stay, having come all the way from Siberia, until about the first week of June. This is why in recent years bird migration along the Norfolk coast during spring has been so poor.

There have been long, cold springs lasting until early June, as in 1975 and 1984; there have been long, mild and very wet ones, as in 1983; and only once I enjoyed a superb spring, the one everyone still remembers, in 1976, a year which saw the gorgeous swallowtail butterfly on the wing daily between 9th May and 24th September.

The first signs at Hickling that spring is on the way come from the swollen pale-grey buds of sallows and osiers, the tender shoots of the reed "colt" peeping through the peat on the marshes, the departure of wintering wild swans and, in the first week of March, the return of the first lapwings, redshank and ringed plovers to grazing marshes and wader pools, where they breed. Certainly one of the finest sights and sounds is that of large groups of Bewick's swans coming over very high from the west, often against a clear blue sky. Undoubtedly they have left the Ouse Washes and Slimbridge, where hundreds of them now winter, and are on their way home via the Low Countries. For me it is a moment of pure magic.

Early March can produce vocal evidence that winter is, hopefully, behind us and spring may not be all that far away. Yellowhammers and reed buntings fill their lungs and produce rather frail songs; a lone blackbird does the same towards the end of a sunny afternoon; peewits tumble and utter loud cries of joy over grazing marshes and wader pools; greylag and Canada geese, on the whole silent during the depths of winter, are now paired off and squabble noisily about the waterways, where splashes of gold on some marshy banks reveal the flowering splendour of marsh marigolds.

Early April sees the arrival of one of my favourite songsters, the willow warbler. From the fifth day onwards, on my early-

A sedge warbler brings food to its nest, buried deep in a fen.
Dr K. J. Carlson

74

morning walks, my ears are tuned to detect that first lovely descending cadence, and when I hear it I hope that spring has really arrived. Other summer visitors soon follow, and it is not long before sedge warblers are chattering away in the reedbeds. Then around the fourteenth day I take a punt silently through certain dykes, straining my ears to catch the first reeling songs of one of our rarest nesting birds, the Savi's warbler. It is strange how its numbers fluctuate from one year to the next. In a good year there may be eight singing males, but in the following year perhaps only one or two. They seem to be oblivious to a man in a punt, for I have watched one singing on the top of a low bush only four yards away. On a perfectly still evening in June I have heard its song over a mile distant, the low-pitched purring sound travelling on the lightest of airs.

The day comes in April when both grasshopper and Savi's warblers are singing within a short distance of each other, while all around them are reed and sedge warblers. Other arrivals by now include yellow wagtails, whitethroats, lesser whitethroats, garden warblers, cuckoos and turtle doves. One winter visitor still dallies with us; I regard the water pipit as a Hickling speciality. In the winter of 1983–84 no fewer than fourteen were present. It is in April when this plump-looking pipit is most handsome; its striking feature is the pinkish-white breast, which is usually unstreaked. In addition the almost uniform slate-grey back and wings, with two prominent white bars, and a conspicuous white eye-stripe are diagnostic. It really is a beautiful bird at this time of year. Its voice, too, is different from that of the resident meadow pipits, but it takes a keen ear and a lot of experience to distinguish the high pitched "*tseep-tseep*" calls of the meadow pipit from the slightly lower-pitched and harsher "*streak-streak*" notes of the water pipit.

Towards the end of the third week in April I eagerly await the return of my favourite bird, the little tern. In most years other terns pass through on their spring migration, Arctic, sandwich, black and roseate terns. Up to sixteen pairs of common terns bred on the reserve each year up to 1986. Both Caspian and white-winged black tern have been recorded.

Seven o'clock on the evening of 14th May, 1980, was notable for the exceptional numbers of black terns crossing the west end of the broad. I was on the lookout enjoying a watch and a listen in perfect weather conditions when through my binoculars I saw many black terns crossing the placid waters at the west end of the broad. During the next half-hour several hundred of these graceful birds approached the broad from the south, and for some time they flew around, dipping down to snatch insects on and over the water. Scores were lost from sight behind Jervis Point, and a day or two later residents on Hill Common told me there was a stream of them passing northwards over their houses. When I left the lookout others were still coming up from the south. Next morning only eleven could be seen.

Swallows, martins and swifts may be seen, sometimes from dawn to dusk, over the marshes and waterways. They begin to arrive in April, and, in the case of swifts, continue to appear well into June. The spring passage movement is hurried and definite; no time is wasted in aerial sport, and not much in feeding. The direction of the wind makes very little difference to them; the maximum numbers are often recorded on the wildest days. The strength and ease of their flight is beautiful to watch. Migration journeys call for little in the way of extra energy where swifts are concerned. They live on the wing all day, and what they do all night is a mystery. Some do say they rest in Heaven. Swifts, it is claimed, are capable of a cruising speed of fifty miles per hour; if that is true a few hours would take them far towards the end of their migration.

Miss E. L. Turner recorded a unique incident concerning a swift on Hickling Broad in 1930:

I seem, so far, to have been the only individual who has seen our common swift perch in a tree. This occurred on September 12th, 1930. A single bird flew to my island at Hickling at 7.20 pm. It circled round the tall willows three times, each time turning over in the air and making a noise with its wings like a lapwing. Then it alighted on a very thin twig and immediately fell asleep. It was still asleep, with its head tucked under one wing, at 7.15 the next morning, but left about 7.45. There had been heavy rain all day on the 12th, and a succession of very strong gales.[1]

The month of May arrives, and we pray for some really warm weather with plenty of sunshine, and winds from the west to bring migrating birds to our side of the country. Sunshine is paramount if we are to see an early emergence of swallowtails; and from the middle of the month onwards the telephone brings calls from all over the country from people wanting to know if they are flying yet. As already mentioned, in the glorious May of 1976 the first was seen on the 9th; but the appallingly cold and cloudy weather in 1984 saw the first one emerge on 13th June.

If we get persistent easterly winds throughout May, which is often the case, then wading birds in particular are very thin on the ground. Families who live in Wales and visit the reserve in May while on holiday tell me what a marvellous spring passage of migrating birds they have had back home, thanks to easterly winds.

May is the month when during warm sunny periods adders can be seen sunning themselves on pathways and on banks beside the dykes. Over the past decade it has been the peak booming time

A sparrowhawk and young at the nest.
Dr K. J. Carlson

for our one or two male bitterns; elsewhere they can be heard from early in March. Eels begin "running" upriver for Heigham Sounds and the broad, and the eel catchers are back in business once again. Their nets are laid close to the reed fringes, so take care you do not get too close with your power-driven boat or you will wind a net round your propeller and be in a lot of trouble.

May is also the only month when, if one is very lucky, all three species of harriers may be seen. Undoubtedly one of the finest and rarest sights in Broadland in spring is the courtship flight of the male marsh harrier, and the holidaymaker moored up in the vicinity of Heigham Sounds, Meadow Dyke or Horsey Mere stands a good chance of witnessing this. One remains unaware that this is going on high above until a sharp "*wick*" cry is heard. With luck the bird may be seen fairly quickly, but often it can be two or three minutes before it is spotted as a mere speck when it passes across a huge white cumulus cloud. At intervals the male bird announces his presence with that penetrating, far-carrying call. His aerial skill is superb. He rolls, pitches, and shoots skywards again, at times almost turning on his back. The wing-beats are immensely strong and deliberate, and at times his wings appear to move in slow motion. These gyrations high in the heavens go on for days, and all the time the female is somewhere about the marshes below him. On a few occasions I have witnessed the conclusion of these aerobatics, when the male tore down out of the sky in a matter of seconds, to level out and make a playful pass at his spouse flying a hundred feet or so above the marsh.

Spring is indeed a most rewarding time of the year.

Some Bird Characters   5

HICKLING is host to many species of bird, as one can see from the list given in appendix one, but there are some birds that are special. These are the inhabitants of wetlands, of reedbeds and marshlands, now confined largely to areas such as the Broads. It is these birds in particular which bring visitors from afar to Hickling.

Bittern

We know from historians that the bittern was hunted during the Stone Ages and that fossil remains have been found in Scotland; in Bronze Age times it was hunted along with the pelican and bustard from the Humber to the Thames.

In more recent times it nested in southern Scotland in the eighteenth and nineteenth centuries until about 1830, and in Ireland during the first half of the nineteenth century. In England it formerly nested in Broadland, in the fens of Norfolk and Cambridgeshire, and in Lancashire and Yorkshire, and it also nested in suitable localities in Wales.

In Norfolk it was already decreasing in numbers by the middle of the nineteenth century, possibly because of the numbers being shot. Writing in 1845, the Rev. Richard Lubbock remarked that it had "decreased much in number in the last twenty years" and went on to say:

> I remember when these birds could be found with certainty in the extensive tracts of reed about Hickling broad and Heigham sounds. Four or five might be seen in a morning.[1]

Mr Lubbock himself seems to have had a hand in reducing the bittern to near extinction, for during a snipe and duck shooting expedition in 1819 he killed eleven bitterns "without searching particularly for them". The last breeding record known to Thomas Southwell, who produced a new edition of Lubbock's *Observations on the Fauna of Norfolk*, was on Upton Broad in 1868, and by 1886 the bittern was no longer known in the Broads[2].

One of the most important dates in ornithological history was 7th July, 1911, for it was on this day that Jim Vincent and Emma Turner found the bittern had returned to breed in Norfolk, at Sutton Broad, to the west of Hickling. From that date it steadily re-established itself in Broadland, and by the mid-fifties it was

Opposite page: *The first European photograph of a female Montagu's harrier and young, taken at Hickling by Niall Rankin on 28th June, 1929.*
J. C. Cadbury

79

estimated that there were at least sixty booming males concentrated about Barton, Hickling and Horsey. Who better to tell us about that memorable day in 1911 than Jim Vincent himself:

Have heard the last few days of Bittern (Common) being seen at Sutton 2 miles from Hickling. Miss Turner and myself asked Mr Robert Gurney, whose ground they were on, about them. He stated he had never seen the bird, but his keeper had, and he gave us permission to go and hunt for them. We arrived about 1.30 pm, and after waiting for some time the bird crossed us, and after flying at least 500 yards. An hour after it returned again, about the same time back it came to the same place. We moved to a position abreast of it, and saw the bird get up and flop above the reeds a few yards. I dived off for a 100 yards into a thick bed of reeds and gladden, principally gladden, up to my thighs in mud and water, and could see where the new gladden was broken, no doubt by the old bittern clutching it upon alighting. When close to where she alighted, heard her quarking away, and flushed her about 5 yards away when she became very noisy and fussy; I searched round, but could see or find nothing whatever. After tea Miss Turner and myself went back, and both went upon my old track, heard the bird talking away and flushed her ahead. I searched round where she got up and found a young one, beak and neck skywards. He was two-thirds grown. Could hardly realize it.

July 8th: Went with Miss Turner at 3 am, found young Bittern and he was photographed in various attitudes. Saw the old bird fly across the reeds twice, and first time of entering the high reeds walked within 10 yards of it, but was guided by the bird uttering its quark, quark, could find no nest, or any other youngsters though I have not the least doubt there are some others, but as it is impossible to see one's way cannot systematically work the ground, and the young could very easily be passed.[3]

Jim Vincent's account is, as one might expect from such a man, a fairly matter-of-fact and unemotional one. Miss Turner's own account of the finding of the infant bittern betrays more of the excitement of the occasion.

From 6.30 to 7.30 we watched from a bank, but as there was no sign of any Bittern we both plunged into the reed-bed, determined to make a thorough search before dark. The water was above our knees, and the reeds were so dense that neither of us could see the other when a few yards apart. We soon put up the old bird, and then Vincent suggested that I should stand still while he worked in circles round me. At last came a joyful shout—"I've got one youngster; come quick"—and I pressed forward headlong in the direction of his voice. How we gloated over our prize as he stood there, transformed into the resemblance of a bunch of reeds! With long pointed bill thrust straight upwards, bright eyes half-closed, the feathers of his head and neck smoothed downwards, so that their alternate dark and light markings blended absolutely with the reeds; the bird's bulky body, owing to its broken-up colouring, seemed absolutely to "melt" into its surroundings; while the big green legs and feet, being partially submerged in water, might easily have been mistaken for reed-stalks.

It was now 8.30 and the sun was setting. What was to be done with the young Bittern now we had found him? I insisted on some third person seeing our captive lest the unbelieving world should scoff; so I carried the wild, beautiful thing to dry land. This was no easy task, for I was almost too excited to hold him, and he could not be tucked under my arm because of sundry fierce thrusts upwards which he made with his bill. We had for the moment lost our "sense of direction," but guided by the sunset glow, we stumbled on and soon hit our trail and emerged triumphant. Then we stowed the bird safely away for the night; and by alternate rowing, cycling, and rowing returned home, finally reaching my houseboat at 10.15. I changed into dry clothes, and, in spite of considerable anxiety, slept soundly until 2 a.m.

We started away again at 3 o'clock, this time provided with wading-boots, cameras, and other necessaries—as much as two bicycles could possibly carry. By 4 a.m. I had the Bittern once more in my arms safe and sound. When I put him on the ground he stalked off in a solemn and what was intended to be a dignified manner. In reality he appeared very ludicrous; for with big green legs and splayed feet, drooping wings and head held high in the air, he looked like a tall, gaunt old woman masquerading in bird's attire. But when put back to his natural surroundings, one saw how this seemingly ludicrous attitude was an instinctive pose tending to self-preservation, and rendering him more or less inconspicuous.

The young bird emitted a curious bubbling note; this can easily be imitated by blowing through a straw into a glass of water, and is quite distinct from the hoarse call-note of the adult bird, which is not unlike that of the Great Crested Grebe, but shorter and sharper. Having finished photographing the young Bittern, we hunted round after the nest; but being anxious for the safety of the bird which now began to "bubble" in a way likely to attract his parents, we gave up the search and left him in peace.[4]

Other bitterns nested in the same locality in the following years, and as numbers increased the bird extended its range. In 1917 a nest containing young bitterns was found at Hickling, and the next year four pairs are known to have bred at Hickling and two at Sutton. In 1923 B. B. Riviere estimated that sixteen or seventeen pairs were breeding in Norfolk, and in his book *A History of the Birds of Norfolk* he expressed the belief that in 1928 the number of breeding pairs had increased to twenty-three or twenty-five, perhaps more.

During the following decade the bittern extended its breeding area beyond the Broadland and in 1937 a pair nested at Cley, on the North Norfolk coast. A survey in 1954 indicated a total for the whole county of sixty booming males, the majority of them in the Hickling, Horsey and Barton areas, but then a decline set in, aggravated by the arctic winter of 1963, which caused a number of losses among the bittern population.[5]

By 1970 the county total had been reduced to twenty-eight booming males, and six years later no more than nine boomers were recorded in Broadland, two of them at Hickling; this Hickling figure might have indicated two or more nesting females. From the mid nineteen-eighties only a single boomer was present, and no breeding is thought to have occurred on the reserve.

The bittern is without doubt the most mysterious and secretive bird in Broadland, and it is the one bird above all others that the many visitors to Hickling want to see. I have lost count of the number of people who, on paying their first visit to the reserve, said "we've come especially to see your bitterns." Sadly, I have had to tell them that the chances of seeing one are very slim indeed. Today we rarely hear two, and usually only one booming male. He is polygamous and we hope he may have one or two nesting females; but we don't investigate closely for fear of disturbing them.

I am certain the bittern's decline is due entirely to the deterioration in water quality. By May the water in the main waterways and dykes around the broad and Heigham Sounds begins to resemble green pea soup, and in most years a white disc is invisible to the human eye three inches below the surface of the water. Surely the bittern must experience equal difficulty in seeing a frog, toad or eel. The many dykes, pools and "holes" in the ronds fringing the major waterways are the quiet, undisturbed places where the bittern hunts its food. Unlike our nesting herons, which breed in a wood close by Heigham Sounds, the bittern does not fly away from these ronds to the clean, clear dykes that divide grazing and arable lands to seek its food.

In 1982 we made three "bittern pools" in a reedbed not far from Meadow Dyke. These are separated from the foul water of the broad by the flood bank. Each one is about a hundred yards long by eight yards wide, with a graduated slope along one side where bitterns can walk through the reeds and feed in water of variable depth.

Although a sighting of a bittern on Hickling is a rare thing today, its foghorn booming may still be heard between March and June. The holidaymaker and his family moored in Meadow Dyke or in Deep-Go-Dyke may have a bird booming less than a hundred yards away. I have sometimes been asked about the noise that has kept them awake most of the night; people find it hard to believe that a bird can make such a sonorous sound for hours on end. During May and June on still warm nights I have lain in bed and listened to a bittern booming nearly two miles distant.

Sadly, the bittern's hold on Hickling today is very tenuous; and

Opposite page: *A female bittern on the nest deep in a reedbed.*
per S. Linsell

in the whole of Broadland in the mid-eighties it was thought there were no more than four booming males. It is a bird which can suffer great losses during prolonged spells of arctic weather; like the heron and kingfisher, it is starved of food if the waterways are frozen over for any length of time. During one spell of hard weather in 1978 I was walking one morning from my house to Whiteslea Lodge when I suddenly noticed a bittern standing beside the dyke bordering the road. It was all hunched up and looked incredibly small, and made no effort to move as I approached. When I was no more than a few yards from it the bittern's head and neck slowly adopted a vertical position. It was obviously almost starved to death; I decided to take it home and try to restore it to good health. That bird taught me a very sound lesson, for as I bent down to pick it up, quick as a flash it jabbed that dagger-like bill straight at my right eye. Fortunately my reaction was pretty quick, and I moved my head just enough; it grabbed the skin above my cheek bone an inch below my eye. Although so starved it would not take fish from me; it died two days later. Ringing recoveries have shown that numbers of Continental winter immigrants arrive in Norfolk, so this could have been a bird from across the North Sea.

Peter Bond excavating the first of three bittern pools made in a reedbed not far from Meadow Dyke in 1982 in an attempt to provide a suitable habitat for these birds. S. Linsell

Very occasionally during spring and summer I have watched a male marsh harrier swooping up and down over a reedbed beside

Heigham Sounds, undoubtedly mobbing a bittern; but I have never witnessed a bittern attacking a marsh harrier, as Lord William Percy did at Hickling back in the early nineteen-thirties, when he spent more than 125 days at different bitterns' nests studying their habits and ways. During all that time he never once saw both male and female bittern together at the nest. In one of his essays he tells us:

> On one occasion when a harrier approached a nestful of young bitterns, the old hen not only rose to meet it, but with agonised cries called the cock bittern to her aid, and amid a chorus of yelps the three birds twisted in the air in such confusion that each appeared alternately the chaser and the chased. There could be little doubt that on that occasion, at least, the intentions of the harrier were not taken on trust.[6]

Miss Emma Turner was also witness to the rare sight of two bitterns fighting in the air, as well as seeing a bittern rising to attack a marsh harrier.

> Occasionally two Bitterns will fight in the air. They then mount in circles and endeavour to swoop down at one another. In these instances one male may be merely driving another away from his breeding area. Undoubtedly Bitterns could put up a considerable fight if they liked, for both beak and claws are powerful weapons. So far I have only seen these fights when the breeding season is at its height, so that they are not part of the spring display. On June 9, 1918, I watched a fight between a Bittern and a Marsh Harrier. I suppose no living ornithologist has hitherto seen such a thrilling sight in the British Isles. I was rather out of heart after a long and fruitless attempt to photograph a Bittern on the wing, and sat in my boat feeling I should like to throw my camera overboard. This attitude of extreme dejection gave place to one of absorbed interest. Looking up I saw a Marsh Harrier approaching the Bittern's nesting area. Slowly and majestically the Harrier swept onwards, ruthlessly disregarding the dismay his presence created amongst the smaller birds of the neighbourhood. Suddenly a Bittern shot up from the reed-bed, and the Harrier only avoided being impaled on the point of the adversary's beak by a dexterous twist. It was a clear June evening, the marshes were bathed in golden light, and everything was sharp and clean cut. High in the air the two birds turned and twisted, the one to all appearances so immeasurably stronger than the other. It looked a very unequal fight. There never seems anything very tangible about Bitterns on the wing, their flight is slow and stately, noiseless almost as that of an Owl; but this bird was transformed into a whirling mass of golden-brown. Furiously it bore down upon its dusky adversary, and its valour was more than a match for the enemy, for the Harrier sheered off closely pursued by the Bittern until both birds were out of sight. By-and-by the Bittern returned and dropped down near the nest.[7]

Another rare sight is a bittern flying at a height of several hundred feet and for a long distance, something I have seen on only two, perhaps three, occasions. One such bird took wing from the south side of Heigham Corner. It climbed in spiralling flight for some time, attaining a height, I guessed, of about 500 feet, and then flew over Hickling village and out of sight. Verily the bittern is a rum owd bird!

Bearded tit

How accurate was B. B. Riviere in describing the bearded tit as the very embodiment of the spirit of the Norfolk Broads. What a superb bird it is, particularly the cock bird with his blue-grey head and black moustache.

It is my great sorrow that in all the years I was at Hickling I never found time to watch a nesting pair with their young—the life of the warden is far too busy for that. On those occasions when I have quietly punted along the reed fringes of the broad, or the Sounds, or pushed the punt silently through remote dykes, I have had unsurpassed views of adult birds only a few feet away; or, later in the summer, the lovely sight of a family playing about the feathery heads of the reeds, "ping"-ing and "phutt"-ing away in a glorious chorus of sound. And then, very rarely, I have been in the right place at the right time to witness a dozen or more take flight together from the bronzed reeds and reedmace; dancing high into the air, they have flown away out of sight in jinking and jerking flight. This happens in late September or October, when they have decided to explore "pastures new" far afield.

Some stay with us throughout the winter, even during spells of arctic weather. Before the harvesting of reed on Hickling became mechanized, with the acquisition of the Olympia reed harvester, it was a regular feature for our marshmen to have a number of bearded tits around their feet while they dressed out the reed. There was also the odd robin and stonechat, likewise on the hunt for insects and grubs. In those days the cut reed was left lying on the marsh until it was dressed out, and the birds were able to get in among the loose reed and search for food.

Next to the bittern, the bearded tit is the bird most visitors to the reserve want to see. You are not likely to see any if the winds are strong, for then they keep to the sheltered bottoms of the reedbeds and rarely call. For a detailed study of this marvellous character let us turn again to Miss Emma Turner, who enjoyed so many years in their company early in the present century:

A Bearded Tit on an April day and beneath an April sky—this is the crowning glory of the marshland. When Nature made the reed-beds, she evolved the Bearded Tit on purpose to play in them.

To see this species in perfection, you must lie up in a punt amongst the reeds on a windless day, late in April. The reed-beds are more beautiful then in their decay than ever they were in their midsummer pride, for the subtle alchemy of the spring sunshine turns their greyness into gleaming gold—tawny gold, the one perfect setting for the tawny little gymnast who presently will slide up the reeds and peep through at you. A quiet day is absolutely necessary, for the Reed Pheasant* is none too robust, and hates being buffeted by the wild wind. His approach is heralded by a sharp metallic note akin to the ping of a bullet or the twanging of a violin string. This is practically his only song, but the note is capable of a modulation, and when rapidly repeated by both sexes, or by several birds together, it has a peculiar resonance which carries a long distance. Soon the bird itself will appear. If the male, he is at once distinguished from the female by his grey head and long black moustaches. Both are clad in russet plumage, which tones with the dead reed-stems. Tawny and grey, the Bearded Tits take on colour from their surroundings according as the reed-beds are illuminated by bright sunlight or fade into greyish-brown under a clouded sky.

At one time the Bearded Tit was in great danger of becoming extinct in the British Isles. But since it has become the object of both public and private protection, this unique denizen of the Broads has increased considerably up to a certain point.

The Reed Pheasant is gregarious in the winter, but from the middle of February onwards the flocks disintegrate, and the males fight furiously. They chase each other over the reeds, and then, dropping into cover, continue the brawl in private.

When courting the hen, the cock erects his grey head feathers and puffs out the two long ends of his beard in a way that is obviously irresistible. The long tail is held erect and fanned, so that the jet black under-coverts are brought into prominence. The female sometimes takes no notice of this display, but merely clings to a reed and looks the other way. Occasionally, however, she executes a curious dance along a comparatively horizontal reed; this dance resembles a minuet in its slow stateliness. At intervals both birds fluff out their contour feathers and fan their tiny wings. Before settling down to family cares a kind of nuptial flight is taken. This is beautiful to watch, and surprising when, as a rule, one only sees these birds flitting somewhat clumsily from cover to cover. Both leave the sheltering reed-beds and, with clear call-note, rise gradually into the air. There is no undue haste when once the couple begin to soar; with outstretched wings and quivering tail, they seem to float upwards. Sometimes the male will be uppermost and sometimes the female, and in this manner they rise alternately until both are mere specks in the blue. You have to watch and watch for the specks to reappear, for the descent is made suddenly and they drop like stones into the reeds, there to take up the burden of life after this excursion into mid-air. And life is a very serious business to the Reedlings, for they may produce and rear fifteen or eighteen young ones in a season.

*Miss Turner points out that Reed Pheasant and Bearded Reedling are Norfolk names for the Bearded Tit.

Occasionally nests will be found amongst low-growing sedges and rushes on a comparatively dry marsh, but the Bearded Tit prefers dense masses of sedge and reed, through which one has to wade ankle-deep or knee-deep in water. It is easy enough to mark down a pair of Reed Pheasants and locate the site of their nursery, but its actual discovery is quite another matter. It is placed low down, sometimes only a few inches above the water-line and amidst the thickest cover, so that it is admirably sheltered from the inclement weather and screened from birds of prey. Predatory humans also have to beware, or they get their hands badly cut by the saw-edged sedges.

The first Reed Pheasant's nest I ever saw was in April, 1901. It was also my very first experience of a reed-bed, and being told to "look", I hastily stepped out of the boat and found myself up to my arm-pits in water. I grasped at the sedges to save myself and the results were disastrous to my hands. However, it was worth it, and I gained wisdom from experience.

I well remember coming one brilliant Sunday morning in May upon three broods of Bearded Tits—fifteen young in all—which were dotted about upon the ooze in one of these secluded spots. Each bird waited in silent expectancy, for they are not boisterous like the young of some species, but patiently await their turn to be served. The air was full of the hum of insect-life. Snipe drummed dreamily, Redshank and Lapwing were calling overhead, and all the smaller songsters filled the waste spaces with their "sweet jargoning". Two of the male Reedlings hawked for flies on the wing, turning and twisting in the sunlight as they chased delicate winged insects. One very beautiful male bird swung on a tall reed eyeing me suspiciously and resentfully, but the three females ran hither and thither regardless of everything but the needs of their respective broods.

Suddenly the hitherto brilliant sun became overclouded, the wind rose, and away over the Broad came the sound of lashing hail upon the open water. In two minutes I was back in my houseboat behind closed doors, while twenty minutes later my man was shovelling away ice from the stern-sheets before the doors could be again opened. I cannot tell what became of the tits. It seems to me that such sudden changes of temperature, together with the tremendous downpour of rain and stinging hail, must surely destroy numbers of half-grown birds. At any rate, I did not see so many Bearded Tits again in that locality. Sudden storms shatter birds' nerves, and inexperienced young cannot be immediately rounded into a place of safety by half-distracted and anxious parents.

After the breeding season, old and young collect together and wander from Broad to Broad. As winter approaches, they may be seen in flocks of from twenty to forty, but—with the exception of a few enterprising stragglers who generally come to a bad end—they do not roam far from their breeding-areas.

In the winter the Bearded Tit's principal food consists of the larvae of *Laverna phragmitella*, which begins to burrow into the reed-mace during August and remains there all the winter, causing the "pokers" to burst out and become fluffy. They also feed upon another grub which

Above: *A swallowtail butterfly, one of the creatures which brings visitors to Hickling.* Dr Alan Beaumont

Right: *Swallowtail caterpillars, whose sole food plant is the milk parsley.* S. Linsell

Below: *Fen flora in high summer. The white flower heads of milk parsley are prominent.* S. Linsell

Left: *An injured bittern found at Whiteslea. Although attempts were made to care for it, the bird later died.* S. Linsell

Below: *The rich colour of the reed shows in this autumn scene.* S. Linsell

bores into the reed stems. It is largely owing to the presence of these two insects that the frail Reedling is able to endure the rigours of a Broadland winter; they need not leave the sheltering reed-beds in search of food. From recent observations made upon the feeding habits of this species, I doubt if it ever devours seeds at all. The fact that there must be plenty of insects amongst the reed-beds in the winter is proved by the presence of innumerable Common Wrens which frequent them throughout the cold months. So tame are they in the winter, that I have sat by a heap of reeds while the men were reed-cutting and watched them picking up insects at my feet. They will follow the reed-cutters all day, feeding in the exposed ooze when the reeds are removed.

The bearded tit is at all times a remarkable gymnast, and performs all kinds of feats amongst the reeds, sliding up and down or twisting round and round a stalk with indescribable dexterity. It seldom comes head-first down a reed, neither does it climb hand over hand. Both the ascent and the descent are made in a series of rapid jerks. Whenever a branching leaf obstructs its way the bird avoids it by slipping round the stalk.

Perhaps, after all, the male Bearded Tit shows to best advantage in the winter. It is then that one so often sees him balanced on a swaying reed-mace remorselessly scattering its fluffy contents as he searches for food. The soft buff and brown of the bird's plumage exactly tones with the torn and ragged "pokers", and his beautiful grey head blends with the wintry sky. Let us leave him swinging there, a perfect master in poise: "The Broads faire ornament and Heaven's glorie—Joy may you have."[8]

Like so many other species, the bearded tit suffered severely at the hands of nineteenth-century collectors. The Rev. Richard Lubbock, who for some unknown reason omitted this bird from his *Observations on the Fauna of Norfolk*, asked a marshman to shoot some bearded tits for him "for preservation" but regretted that when he received them they were spoilt by being killed with large shot. He supplied the marshman with dust shot, and as a result received six birds killed at one shot.[9] Egg collectors, too, contributed to a decline in the species, which at one time was so numerous that Henry Stevenson in his *The Birds of Norfolk* wrote of them flying up "simultaneously soon after sunrise, swarming for awhile like a flock of bees" in autumn.

Stevenson commented on the problems faced by the species:

It is greatly to be regretted that the demand for specimens from their handsome plumage should lead to the wholesale slaughter of the Bearded Tits throughout the winter; added to which, the price of late years offered for their eggs has caused a sensible diminution in their numbers. After the mild winter of 1862–3, these birds were more than usually plentiful at Hickling in the following spring, and from this locality alone about five dozen eggs were procured by one individual, nominally a collector, but in reality a dealer, who thus for the sake of a few shillings would go far towards exterminating this beautiful species

(many old birds being also killed at the time), whose numbers we have no reason to suppose are replenished by continental migrants. Already in one or two districts, where only a few years back they were very plentiful, scarcely a pair or two to my knowledge can now be found in the breeding season.[10]

In spite of Stevenson's strictures on the trade, the traffic in both birds and eggs seems to have continued unchecked. A well-known dealer at Yarmouth received no fewer than 113 bearded tit eggs between 10th and 25th April, 1876. Small wonder that Jimmy Nudd, then keeper on the Hickling estate, reckoned in 1889 that there were no more than two pairs nesting on Hickling Broad and Heigham Sounds[11].

The bearded tit became a protected species in 1895 and in this century began to increase its numbers. Whereas in 1899 Mr J. H. Gurney had estimated that there were only thirty-three nests scattered over twenty-two broads, Miss Turner wrote that in 1909 she knew of seventeen nests in about a fifth of the area of one large swamp alone. In *Broadland Birds* she pointed out that the number of breeding birds varied considerably from year to year, for the bearded tit is particularly vulnerable to bad weather:

> After a mild winter, followed by a correspondingly mild spring, Bearded Tits' nests will be plentiful. But after a hard winter or a cold spring, their numbers will be considerably reduced. Even a few days of really severe weather late in the season will produce dire results.[12]

A prolonged spell of bad weather during the winter of 1916–17 decimated the bearded tit population, and in 1920 Miss Turner saw only two broods of fledged young roosting in a reedbed which had formerly sheltered three times that number. When B. B. Riviere published his *A History of the Birds of Norfolk* in 1930 he recorded that the bearded tits' principal stronghold was in the area of Hickling Broad, Whiteslea, Heigham Sounds and Horsey Mere, where Jim Vincent estimated that there were between fifteen and thirty pairs, depending on the severity or mildness of the preceding winter.

The population received another severe setback in the winter of 1947–48. After the blizzards of that winter a single male at Hickling was apparently the sole survivor in Norfolk, yet two pairs returned to nest at Hickling in 1948 and over the succeeding years numbers again built up. In his *Birds of Norfolk*, published in 1967, Michael Seago records that the county population reached more than 130 pairs in 1964 and 1965, probably higher than at any time during the last century. More than a hundred of those pairs were in the Hickling–Horsey–Martham area[13].

During the month of May each year a census was carried out at Hickling of the number of breeding pairs, an operation in which

Opposite page: *A male bearded tit feeding its young. This bird is the very embodiment of the spirit of the Norfolk Broads.* Dr K. J. Carlson

93

James Cadbury used to give me a helping hand, for which I was always most grateful. During my first six years on the reserve we usually arrived at a figure of about 110 pairs, indicating that the species was holding its own in a most satisfactory way. Sadly, during the nineteen-eighties we had a succession of hard winters followed by prolonged cold springs which hit the bearded tit hard, and numbers have been drastically reduced as a result. In 1987 we counted only twenty-three pairs, but thanks to three consecutive mild winters followed by warm springs the population has improved since that time.

The best place from which to see this lovely bird these days is from the public footpath along the Potter Heigham wall.

Little tern

Until I came to Hickling I do not think I had ever had a "favourite" bird, but once I was established there I realized that a very special bird had come into my life—the lesser or little tern, which is the symbol of the Norfolk Naturalists' Trust.

Historians tell us there are no records of the little tern occurring in Britain before 1661, but in 1845 the Rev. Richard Lubbock recorded that he had found the nests of both "Lesser and Common Terns" on an island in Hickling Broad, though it appears from what he says that they had by 1845 ceased to breed there. Mr Lubbock tells us that the terns were known on the Broads as "dars", the common tern being simply a "dar" and the lesser tern the "little dar"; the black tern which he refers to as having been formerly very abundant was the "blue dar".

Writing of the terns in his book *Observations on the Fauna of Norfolk*, Mr Lubbock seems himself to have had a soft spot for the little tern:

> The smallest species, the Lesser Terns (*Sterna minuta*) are very engaging little birds: in the summer time they will fly backwards and forward over a boat moored for angling. I have often been attended by them at Hickling and Horsey. They approach within a very few yards, and are highly delighted with a very small fish—on one or two occasions, when I had minnows with me, they came close to the boat to take them. All these birds are now with us hardly to be considered more than visitors; their nesting places have been broken up by the incursions of man.[14]

Mr Lubbock goes on to record that one of the rarest of the British terns, the white-winged black tern, had occurred in Norfolk several times. One was killed on Hickling Broad on 27th June, 1867, and on 30th May, 1873, five were shot by Edward Booth out of a flock of seven on Hickling Broad[15].

Is it any wonder that in 1879 Henry Stevenson remarked that

the tern, which "up to the commencement of the present century, bred in hundreds both in the broads and in the fens of Norfolk, has ceased to do so of late years, through the combined effects of drainage and persecution". He added that the last nest of the black tern which he knew of in Norfolk was found at Sutton, near Stalham, in 1858, "when I regret to say the old birds were shot by a marshman, who brought them with two eggs to the late Mr Sayer, a birdstuffer of Norwich, and they are now in my collection"[16].

This beautiful little "sea swallow" reaches our shores from Africa in the second or third week in April. Its breeding sites are scattered along the sandy beaches of these islands, but in 1949 eleven pairs made history by nesting on a rarely exposed island at Abberton reservoir, about two miles from the Blackwater estuary; this was the first inland nesting by this species in Britain this century. It is of particular interest, as will be seen in a moment, that those eleven pairs did not choose sandy or gravelly areas on the island to nest but areas where mud and grass had dried out.

On 18th April, 1975, two pairs arrived on Hickling Broad and soon settled down to nest on a muddy island at Rush Hills, the top inch or so having dried out after being submerged all winter. They simply scraped a shallow depression, added a few small bits of dead vegetation, and then laid their two eggs. The only little terns known to have nested inland in Britain since those at Abberton in 1949, these two pairs each raised one young to the flying stage.

With the arrival of 1976 I could not wait for April. Would the terns come back again? On the 21st a single bird arrived. By May

The muddy islands at Rush Hills provided a nesting place for the little terns in 1975 and succeeding years.
S. Linsell

7th sixteen were present, but even this remarkable number was surpassed on the 13th when forty-two were counted. However, most of these moved on and only three pairs remained to nest. Disappointingly only two young survived and flew away.

The next year will always remain in my memory both because of the weather in May and because of the record numbers of little terns—and also because of egg thieves. The first bird was not seen at Hickling that year, 1977, until 27th April because the terns were held up by adverse weather; that is the latest date of arrival, up to the present.

On 2nd May the wind blew strongly from the east, perishingly cold. Gales which blasted the Norfolk beaches for many days caused severe sandstorms, and the breeding colony of little terns on the beaches between Horsey and Winterton was unable to tolerate such conditions.

The result was that on 21st May no fewer than fifty-two little terns arrived at Rush Hills, where two pairs had begun nesting just a few days earlier. The next two or three days were nail-biting ones for us at Hickling: would these birds stay to breed? By 5th June twenty-two pairs had made their shallow nests in the dried mud and were sitting; four days later another four pairs had joined them. What a successful year that proved to be, for no fewer than forty young flew away—a truly remarkable percentage of the young that hatched. And this despite a visitation by several men intent on stealing the terns' eggs.

The following year, 1978, I counted a record number of little terns, seventy-two, on Rush Hills on 29th May. During June there were forty-one pairs incubating eggs, and on 30th June I counted seventy hatched young. Then tragedy struck: three inches of rain fell over the next few days and on 7th July only twenty chicks could be seen; these twenty in due course flew away.

Next year we had a staggering 122 adult birds present on 11th May, but many of these moved on. Thirty-three pairs remained to nest, and on 29th June I counted forty young. I was bitterly disappointed on my return from a week's holiday to find only two young present on 8th July; there had obviously been heavy predation, but what was responsible? Kestrel, barn owl, heron, or possibly stoat? It could even have been moorhen, for I have witnessed this bird on more than one occasion take eggs, or very young chicks, of redshank and lapwing.

The story of this unique colony of little terns now becomes a gloomy one. In 1980 the number of nesting pairs slumped to eighteen, but nevertheless all seemed well with them. Water levels were low and the weather was kind. As in previous years, the large summering population of mostly immature greater and lesser black-backed gulls and herring gulls caused neither predation nor worry to the terns. Noble volunteers who kept a twenty-four hour watch over Rush Hills never witnessed any predation. So why during June that year did the terns slowly but surely give up incubation? Each day saw fewer and fewer sitting, until only three remained in front of the hide; fifteen pairs had abandoned the main colony.

Then on 20th June I was in the hide when a marsh harrier flew over and, as usual, put every bird in the air. Every bird, that is, except one—an adult lesser black-backed gull, which remained sitting on the ground fairly close to the main nesting site of the terns. Very odd, as I said to the visitors I had with me. This bird was then almost lost from view as about another 300 gulls settled around it. I left my visitors in the hide and walked across the slad; that gull had been incubating two eggs. The only record of this species breeding in Norfolk, and it had to choose Rush Hills!

That gull knew, of course, that the little tern chicks would provide an abundant supply of food for its own young; and the terns themselves knew there was no future in continuing to incubate their eggs. I destroyed the gull's eggs, and in due course

The warden and his helpers preparing one of seven shingle islands on Cadbury's Pool in 1982 in an attempt to attract little terns from Rush Hills. **Eastern Daily Press**

five tern chicks from the three remaining nests fledged and flew away.

During the winter of 1980–81 I made a few shingle and sand islands on Chapman's and Deary's pools, which are separated from the broad by the flood bank and where water levels can be controlled; I hoped these would attract little terns away from Rush Hills. In 1981 only five pairs arrived, of which two nested on Rush Hills, only to be washed out by rising water; two pairs nested on Deary's and two young eventually flew; the fifth pair nested on Chapman's, but lost their young to some predator.

In the winter of 1981–82 the four-acre marsh which separated Chapman's and Deary's was excavated and seven large shingle and sand islands made, as well as several natural ones. Every year since then until 1986 a few pairs nested on the various pools, but there has been no return to the halcyon days of the late seventies, when some interesting observations were made on these lovely sea swallows nesting close in front of the Rush Hills hide.

Normally the female lays two eggs, but very occasionally three are laid. There is a lapse of twelve hours or so between the hatching of each egg, so when three eggs are laid the first two chicks to hatch out have a head start on the third. During the first week of their life all the young are fed on water shrimps caught around the broad, and then the parents begin flying the four miles to the coast to catch their favourite food, sand-eels and whitebait; they fly the four miles back again with one fish for one chick. At this point they ignore the third and youngest chick, which is also the weakest, and it soon dies from starvation. Obviously the parents realize they could not cope with having to feed three young, with a journey of eight miles involved each time. It really was distressing to see the neglected youngster crying for food and not getting any. I did try hand-feeding one of these at home with whitebait, but it just would not take the food.

There was a day I remember in early June, 1978. I was in the hide watching many very young chicks being fed when a thunderstorm approached. Minutes later one of the heaviest hailstorms I have ever seen lashed Rush Hills. As sizable hailstones began falling some parent birds flew in and brooded their young; but other parents were hunting for food along the coast, and their young had no protection at all against the fury of the storm. I felt there was no chance of these little balls of fluff surviving such a battering, which lasted fully ten minutes; for a time the ground was white with hail about half an inch deep, and many chicks lay motionless among it. I felt sure they were dead, but remarkably not one was killed.

A last word on my favourite bird. I think my most gratifying moment was at seven o'clock one morning on Deary's, where a pair had successfully raised their two young, which for many days had been taking longer and longer flights around the area. On this morning the whole family was present. The parents appeared strangely agitated and restless, continually flying about and calling noisily to the two youngsters on the ground. Suddenly the young birds flew up and joined their parents, and I realized they were leaving me. Together they flew north towards the coast and the sea, getting smaller and smaller until I could see them no more. They had gone. As I left the hide I prayed they would all come back to me next year.

The harriers

William Turner (1500–1568), who is considered to be the father of British ornithology, was familiar with the marsh harrier. His references to it in his *Avium Praecipuarum*, the first printed bird book, published in Cologne in 1544, are recognized as the first in literature.

The Rev. Richard Lubbock commented in 1845 that the marsh harrier "might twenty years back have been termed the Norfolk Hawk, it was so generally dispersed amongst the broads".

> Almost every pool of any extent had its pair of these birds; they consumed the day in beating round and round the reeds which skirted the water; this was done for hours incessantly. All the birds wounded by the sportsman fell to the share of the Moor Buzzard. He was, as it were, the *genius loci*, the sovereign of the waste; but, although still often to be met with, he has, like all his congeners, receded before the gun of the gamekeeper—the curse of his race is upon him.[17]

The marsh harrier was formerly known as a summer visitor to Wales, Scotland and Ireland as well as to England, but shooting virtually exterminated it, and by 1878 it had ceased to nest in Britain. Between 1878 and 1926 there were no more than half a dozen breeding records, all from East Anglia, and then during the two following decades up to four pairs nested each year in the Hickling–Horsey–Martham area. Between 1948 and 1959 there were up to six pairs nesting in the same area, but after 1959 the harrier nested at Hickling no more until 1976, my first full year on the reserve. Not that I was in any way responsible for their return!

The pair that nested then in the north-east of the reserve on the north side of the Hundred Acres Marsh, near the Stubb Mill outlet dyke, successfully raised three young, and it was a fine sight to see them on the wing over the reedbeds. The following year the cock bird took two wives, and both nested; between them they raised five young birds to the flying stage.

In 1978 Anglia Water spent the first two months of the nesting

season carrying out extensive works not far from where one female harrier had nested the previous year; although the same bird returned to the area she never settled down. The other female again nested successfully, but after that there was again a gap in the breeding record. One female showed every sign of nesting in 1979 and 1980 in one of the original areas, and in both years I was sure she was happily settled; then trespassers were seen in the vicinity and she disappeared.

No more harriers attempted to breed at Hickling until 1985, when two pairs raised six young to the flying stage, to the delight of thousands of visitors. The following year adult birds were present, but inexplicably no breeding occurred. Happily, in 1987 two pairs returned and each successfully raised two young, and since then one or two pairs have nested each year.

More and more of these beautiful birds have bred in East Anglia in recent years in reedbeds only a fraction the size of those at Hickling. In some areas they have nested in cornfields, as they do on the Continent. It has been said that our reed harvesting at Hickling causes disturbance to the birds when they are prospecting for nest sites, but such activities have not put them off in the years they have bred. Indeed, old marshmen say that in years past they sometimes wielded their scythes and loaded bundles of reed into their lighters not far from where a marsh harrier had settled down to nest without causing the bird to desert. In any case, there are several quiet places at the west end of the reserve and around Heigham Sounds, far away from any reed harvesting activity, which seem entirely suited to the harriers' needs; yet year after year they are ignored by the birds. I remain baffled!

We may have had no regular nesting marsh harriers on the reserve, but Hickling and Horsey are probably the only places in Britain where it is possible to see all three species of harrier in the air at the same time. Jim Vincent recorded that he observed all three birds in the air together on several occasions, but I have been fortunate enough to do so on only three days at the beginning of May.

The female hen harrier is smaller than the marsh harrier but larger than the Montagu's harrier, which she much resembles, and with which she is often confused. The hen harrier has broader wings, and its wing-beat and flight are not so buoyant as that of the female Montagu's. The female hen harrier works closer to the ground or tops of rushes and reeds than either of the other two harriers, and maintains this low method of working after the manner of a sparrowhawk. It possesses more dash and drive than either of the other two species.

Undoubtedly Jim Vincent was THE expert of his day on harriers, and some of his observations noted in 1937 reflect his

Reed harvesting in years gone by proved no deterrent to marsh harriers when they sought a nest site. J. Kime

wide knowledge. It is interesting to read his references to human disturbance with regard to what I have already said about this:

In this season [1937], for the first time in living memory a Marsh Harrier wintered here. She—for it was a young female—belonged to one of the two broods reared here during the previous spring. She was a dark chocolate-coloured bird, and succeeded in picking up a living even during a severe cold spell. One day I saw her flying in a snowstorm. She mated with a male this spring, but though he fed her, no eggs were laid. This leads me, after many years' experience with the Marsh Harrier, to the conclusion that both sexes must be two years old before they breed.

The Marsh Harrier is the largest of the three species of harriers which occur in the British Isles, and at all times is the most easy to distinguish, though both sexes possess a wider range of plumage than the other two species. The Marsh Harrier has been more common here at Hickling during the last ten years than it was sixty years ago—at least, so I judge from information supplied to me by my father. As with the Montagu's Harrier, a price was on its head for collections; and though it came sparingly, it rarely had a chance to breed, as it was the easiest of all harriers to shoot or trap with eggs.

My earliest recollection of this species was of single birds turning up, chiefly females, and the bulk of them immatures. These large chocolate-brown harriers, working over the tops of reeds around the edges of broads and meres, could be seen in this flat country at a great distance. Males, especially adult males, were exceedingly rare. The first one I saw was 26 years ago, and I was puzzled by its strange plumage, which was entirely new to me. The Marsh Harrier comes to us from the Continent early in March, and there is no hard-and-fast rule as to which sex comes first; but the arrivals of females before males have been the more frequent. It is the most noticeable of all the harriers, for the females catch your eye by their slow, laboured flight as they rise and fall on the skyline. They give a few wing beats, then with an upward poise of both wings they glide along.

A sure sign that the arriving birds intend to breed is when the male calls from far overhead. High in the air, a mere speck in the sky, his cry of *wick!* comes down very clearly, for it is a penetrating, far-carrying call. Then he displays his aerial skill. He rolls, pitches, and shoots upwards, almost turning on his back. These gyrations go on for days, and often the female may be seen flying low across the marshes whilst her lord and master performs above.

This breeding call-note of the male I first heard in 1915, and I was ignorant then that it was a sure sign of breeding. But as the days passed things began to look hopeful, and early one morning I saw the male carrying long, streaming material into a rough sedge marsh; then the female assisted, and tarried longer at the nest. Further observations justified my hopes, and on May 24th I felt I must have a peep at the nest. It was a new one to me, and it is always a thrill to see a new nest for the first time, and so I waited until the male brought food, and when his mate came off, I made a bee-line for the nest; but the male flew down

101

upon it. When I arrived at the spot the male rose—and there was the large nest, placed almost 3 feet high in the thick sedge and containing two eggs. Three more were laid later, making a clutch of five.

My employer, the late Lord Lucas, came home on leave, and dashed down to see the sight, for he adored the birds of prey. As we sat on the grassy bank and saw the Marsh Harrier go down to its nest on our right hand, and on our left a Montagu's Harrier settle on her eggs, his lordship turned to me with a sparkle in his eyes, and said, "By Jove! Jim, this is the next greatest sight to the War."

The late J. H. Gurney also came to see the nest. The day was windy, and as we stood within 12 feet of the nest, we could see the silver-grey tail of the male sticking out in an opening of the sedge. We had to wait six years for a second nest, in which were laid two eggs, and whence two young ones fled; and another six years for a third nest, which proved to contain only infertile eggs. But in 1928 two or three pairs nested, and every year since then have done so without a break, down to the present time. As I pen these lines (May, 1937) we have a female on five eggs, guarded by watchers, and as far as I can gather the only one in Norfolk and the British Isles.

The bird is not guarded entirely because of egg-collectors, but because this hawk has nested so close to where the pleasure-craft pass that if one moored dead opposite, the bird might be kept off her eggs for a long period. Not only has this rare bird of prey sought the company of the yachting fraternity, but a Bittern has nested so close to the stream that the end of a yacht boom swings over it; and on the opposite side a Pochard goes off her nest when the yacht tacks over, likewise a Bearded Tit leaves her nest as the sides of a cruising vessel brush past the sedge she is in.

The food of the Marsh Harrier is very varied, comprising the Shovelers, Garganeys, Teal, Moorhens, young Coot, Snipe, Redshank, Lapwings, and the young of Mallard and all ground-nesting birds, including Pheasants. The Marsh Harriers adore leverets, but rarely take young rabbits, though these are plentiful. Barn rats, stoats or weasels, I have never known to be taken, and only once have I seen the birds carrying either an eel or a viper.

The young Marsh Harriers quickly grow into bold, courageous youngsters, and show fight by turning on their backs to use their powerful talons if one's hand goes too near. When nearly fledged they look splendid in their chocolate-brown plumage and buff forehead, and with wings fully extended, remind one of small eaglets. After a few days of short, awkward flights in the vicinity of the nest, they go forth on longer excursions, and soon learn the art of catching food. After leaving us, I fear most of them fall a prey to indiscriminate sportsmen. Even here we find it hard to keep the Marsh Harrier going as a breeding species, also the Montagu's Harrier; though both exist to-day on the sanctuary which I supervise, thanks to incessant care and unceasing watchfulness.[18]

The hen harrier is only a winter visitor, and the first bird is not usually seen until about 10th October—that is my average date over the years. It is not uncommon to see four or more in the air at the same time soon after first light, when they fly across the reserve from their nightly roost. Around the time of sunset I have seen up to a dozen hen harriers flying to their roost, and with them there usually go several merlins. Rather a fine sight!

In winter young birds of the previous breeding season, as well as adult females, are collectively referred to as "ringtails", for they are very difficult to tell apart at a distance. All have the diagnostic white rump, visible at long range. These "ringtails" always out-number the beautiful adult males, with their overall blue-grey colouring and black tips to the wings. While one or more "ringtails" are seen daily throughout the winter over Hickling, I probably see a male no more than half a dozen times in a month. Most birds have departed for their northern breeding grounds by mid-April; but one may stay around until late April, or even the first few days in May, when the first migrant Montagu's harrier turns up.

The Montagu's last nested in the Hickling–Horsey area in 1956, and it is now a fairly regular bird of passage. During my time 1983 was its best year, with no fewer than ten days of sightings. And September, 1984, is memorable for the way in which a young Montagu's appeared to keep constant company with a young marsh harrier. On several occasions I saw them together near Whiteslea—one moment flying close together, and then making playful passes at each other as they twisted and turned in the air with legs outstretched. Oh, if only the Montagu's would return to nest with us!

No wonder Jim Vincent loved his harriers; let us leave the last word about the Montagu's to him:

My recollections of the Montagu's Harrier go back over forty years, to a time when birds in glass cases were the craze, and collections of skins were being made by a number of gentlemen, likewise collections of eggs. These people provided a ready market for both birds and eggs. A good male was worth 20 shillings, whilst the eggs commanded as much as £1 per egg. All this appears horrible to-day, but at that time you were considered a poor ornithologist unless you had shot a few rare species of birds or took rare clutches of eggs.

Prior to 1910, I knew of only two instances in which Montagu's Harriers nested and succeeded in hatching young, and in both instances the nestlings were taken for private collections. To make matters more difficult for the harriers, at that time their nesting-area was much more limited than it is to-day. Before the motor-car came, London and all our towns and cities had tens of thousands of horses which had to be fed; hence the majority of the marshes around the Broads, which were not fed down by cattle, were cut for fodder and bedding by an army of marshmen with their scythes. One of my earliest recollections is of seeing scores of Yellow Wagtails following in the wake

103

of the marshmen and catching the insects disturbed by them as they mowed the grass.

Horses now being comparatively scarce, it is no longer worth while cutting this herbage, with the consequence that there are now hundreds more acres available for the harriers to nest in. But the great growth of rank grasses and so on that has ensued is not so favourable for small ground-nesting birds. The species which were abundant forty years ago are not so numerous now, with the result that the harriers have to range far and wide for their food-supply. The rough herbage area of forty years ago in our neighbourhood comprised that known as Horsey Brayden Marshes, and every Montagu's Harrier that came focussed upon this area. About 1906, approximately, there was an awakening amongst a number of naturalists as to the need to protect the rarer species in our Broadland area, but I must admit that the natives at first looked upon these persons as more fit for a lunatic asylum.

In the many recent photographic records of the Montagu's Harrier, one often sees females of a reddy-brown type and with a dark eye, whereas the adult female possesses a yellow iris and her greyish-brown plumage is splashed with light golden-buff. In our efforts to establish this graceful bird of prey during the last 26 years, we have had to pay the price in seeing the ground-nesting species go down before it. Yellow Wagtails, which were so numerous that they were like marsh marigolds on certain areas, have completely disappeared, so that in 1936 it was impossible to locate a single pair in the entire parish of Hickling. Another change has come over our bird-population since protection of the harriers, and that is that the Redshanks which were scattered over the marshes have now come to nest under the protection of the Lapwings, which are fine policemen to drive the harriers away from their nesting-area. The Redshank is clever enough to realise this, and nests very often within a few feet of the Lapwing. Recently I have noted that the Skylark also likes to nest under the protection of the Lapwing, and only last season I found four Skylarks' nests on the same marsh near four Lapwings' nests.

With all this upset, depletion, and readjustment of the bird-population, I have come to a definite conclusion that too many birds of prey on any bird-sanctuary is not good policy. There is room for them all, but in their proper proportions. I like to see a limited number of harriers, and no one feels more than I that any season is incomplete unless the Montagu's Harriers adorn our marshes.[19]

Some Red-letter Days   6

MANY people telephone the reserve to ask what they are likely to see when they visit the Hickling Broad reserve. It is not easy to give an answer, for one never knows what unusual bird might turn up, but an early morning walk around the reserve will have given the warden sufficient information to make a sensible reply.

Certainly Hickling is one of the best places in Britain for seeing birds, and there are few days in the year when the visitor will be altogether disappointed. On a really good day it is possible to identify more than a hundred different species if one knows what to look for and where to look.

Glancing through my diaries, I have extracted some particularly noteworthy entries which give an idea of the great variety of birds to be seen.

20th April, 1977

A sharp frost in the night had frozen all wader pools and some of the less sheltered dykes. The north-east wind has been very cold all day despite a maximum temperature of 57°F and the sun shining most of the day. Visibility good.

First thing this morning a pair of ring ouzels were in the garden uttering loud "*chack-chack*" calls. Four marsh harriers were in the air near our east boundary, and the first lesser whitethroat singing its head off in the icy conditions! While I was watching the harriers a barn owl came into view. En route to Chapman's and Deary's pools a single swallow and two sand martins flew west; willow and sedge warblers were singing in several areas. Linnets were seen to be paired off. Despite the two pools being frozen over, mallard, teal, gadwall, shoveler, shelduck, ringed plover, dunlin, redshank, snipe, lapwing, one ruff and three yellow wagtails were all here.

The main waterways were clear of ice, so took a punt down the Sounds, where there was a red-throated diver, cormorants, wigeon, pochard, tufted duck, Canada geese paired-off, great crested grebes, and fine views of an early Montagu's harrier. Bearded tits were very vocal. Then pushed my way to the pools in the broad where, in addition to the wildfowl and waders already seen, found a female pintail, two black-tailed godwits, little ringed plover, spotted redshank, oystercatcher, five ruffs and reeves, four Scandinavian lesser black-backed gulls, black-headed, common and herring gulls, and the first common tern and house martin.

During the morning two grasshopper warblers and three cuckoos were heard. Marsh marigolds make a fine splash of colour near the Lodge. This evening went round Skoyles Marsh and noted blackcap, whitethroat, turtle dove, long-tailed and willow tits, great spotted woodpecker, and flying high northwards went six whimbrel. Very vocal.

Richard Butler telephoned to say he had walked the Potter Heigham wall this morning and recorded chiffchaff, many sedge and willow warblers, several redpolls, two marsh tits and three marsh harriers.

The first two or three weeks in April are normally fairly quiet, and the above is an average sample of what may be seen; but in some years the northward migration of waders occurs earlier than in others, which happened in 1982.

21st–23rd April, 1982

In addition to most of the species mentioned above the following were observed over these three days: a crane, bittern, two drake garganey, eleven bar-tailed godwits, several grey plover, little stints, greenshanks, green sandpipers and turnstones, a sanderling, 44 ruffs, no fewer than sixteen white wagtails, pied flycatcher, about 400 fieldfares, two Savi's warblers, a short-eared owl and a sparrowhawk.

The month of May can usually be relied on to produce one or two rarities, such as purple heron, little egret, black-winged stilt, broad-billed sandpiper and Temminck's stint. In most years one or more grey-headed wagtails appear during the last week. If it is a warm and sunny month swallowtails will emerge.

12th May, 1979

Young marsh harriers adopt a threatening posture at an intruder's approaching the nest. These youngsters, photographed in 1976, were the first to be reared at Hickling for nineteen years. S. Linsell

A fine but rather hazy day with a light south-westerly wind; warm with temperature rising to 70°F. Visibility fair. The early morning walk at 0500 hours produced two spoonbills rising from Chapman's; they disappeared eastwards, but at 1700 hours two birds returned to the same pool. One had an orange ring on its left leg. A bittern was booming strongly some distance east of the Lodge, where two adult male marsh harriers were soaring. Many more reed warblers present today, and two Savi's reeling near Whiteslea.

Several grasshopper warblers heard, as well as cuckoos and turtle doves.

Took the punt to the broad pools and was well rewarded with a drake garganey, three little gulls, two of them adults, six wood sandpipers, numerous little stints and two Temminck's, three knots, two grey plover, several spotted redshanks, a sanderling, turnstone, curlew-sandpiper, black-tailed godwit, six greenshank, two bar-tailed godwits, numerous common and green sandpipers, and a little ringed plover, plus the commoner waders. Also, five pairs common tern and no fewer than 108 little tern, and two male blue-headed wagtails.

Around the broad thirty-four black terns were counted, and many bearded tits were seen and heard. A pair of marsh harriers was in the vicinity of Ling's Mill. The one pair of greylags had hatched out their seven eggs and the family were seen steaming in line ahead for Deep Dyke, being buffeted by waves from passing cruisers. A surprise was an immature shag on one of the channel posts, while a few cormorants, including one "southern" form, stood on other posts.

Visitors and myself recorded ninety-seven bird species today.

16th–18th May, 1984

Day after day in the middle of this month my diary reads: "strong and very cold north-easterly winds continue to plague us." Temperatures struggled to reach the mid-50s F. by day, while by night they were repeatedly, and unbelievably, no higher than 40°F. Yet despite the almost wintry conditions there was no shortage of birds.

Don Tate, who then lived at the "Smea" on the west shore of the broad, rang up to inquire if I had seen the eagle over the broad. I told him I hadn't, much to my sorrow; and then later that day the warden at Woodbastwick telephoned to say a white-tailed eagle had left there on a northerly course at 1530 hours, and had I seen anything of it? I told him I hadn't, but somebody else had. Very sadly, the same bird was shot not many miles away a few days later.

The following day a long-eared owl and a pair of ring ouzels were seen, and a pair of little ringed plovers were mating and scraping on the gravel slad. Ruffs were displaying beautifully on Swim Coots and a drake goldeneye was on the broad. At 1845 hours a party of us were on the tree tower in Whiteslea Wood when a male red-footed falcon landed nearby, affording us superb views. Not far away a Cetti's warbler was singing.

The following day, the 18th, was unbelievably cold, but it did not stop birds passing through in considerable numbers—swallows, wheatears, whinchats, a wryneck, turtle doves and swifts; over

Invading alder and silver birch can be seen in this view of Hickling Broad from the tree tower in Whiteslea Wood, whose oaks are prominent in the foreground. Scrub clearance on the former grazing marshes is one of the major management tasks on the reserve.
Dr Alan Beaumont

109

twenty species of waders were recorded, including avocets, sanderlings, grey plovers, turnstones, both Temminck's and little stints, wood and curlew-sandpipers, and whimbrel; while a school party had fine views of two spoonbills and six little gulls. In the evening six black-tailed godwits put in a brief appearance.

During those three days 109 bird species were recorded.

18th June, 1982

A mainly fine and sunny day with a fresh south-easterly wind. Maximum temperature 64°F. Visibility good.

The early morning walk took me to Deary's pool, where the pair of little terns had hatched out their three eggs. While I was in the west hide a brood of six young shovelers swam along the dyke in front. On Cadbury's pool the pair of avocets continue to incubate and the family of oystercatchers continues to do well, as do broods of lapwing, ringed plover and redshank. An interesting bit of behaviour by a grasshopper warbler was noted: a bird landed on the pathway in front of me with its beak full of food, ran mouse-like ahead of me, gently fluttering its wings, and then disappeared into the dense vegetation beside the path. It was not seen again.

A long-eared owl at its nest near Whiteslea.
Dr K. J. Carlson

On the Skoyles Marsh trail willow warblers, blackcap, garden warbler, reed and sedge warblers, whitethroats and lesser white-throat, redpolls, turtle doves and cuckoos were either seen or heard. A female Montagu's harrier, first seen near the Lodge, has stayed around all day, to the delight of visitors.

During the morning David, Harry and Peter arrived on their annual pilgrimage and I boated them around the broad. On Rush Hills we found a Kentish plover in close company with two little ringed plovers, two grey plovers, two little stints, a common sandpiper, greenshank and a whimbrel. Also, a few mallard, teal, shoveler, gadwall, two drake wigeon, twenty-two shelduck, five pairs of little terns, fifteen pairs of common terns, and two little gulls.

When we left here we headed for Swim Coots. En route three broods of pochard and the first brood of tufted duck were seen, and good views were had of a male marsh harrier. As usual great crested grebe broods are reduced to one. Do our few pike take them, or do most of them die from natural causes? On Swim Coots we found two broods of Canada geese and one of shelduck, sixteen herons, nearly all juveniles, four spotted redshank, two wood sandpipers, two greenshank, a black-tailed godwit, plus the commoner waders.

There are fine spreads of climbing corydalis and ragged robin just now, and swallowtails are enjoying the latter.

Late this evening took the punt out and found six Savi's warblers in song, and an unexpected sight was eight avocets flying up the Sounds. As I got back to Whiteslea seven curlew flew high westwards, very vocal.

18th July, 1980

A little rain early this morning, then cloudy with sunny periods; maximum temperature 70°F; visibility good.

The early walk at 0500 hours produced a nice variety on the pools: a few mallard, teal, shoveler and gadwall, and two shelduck; also, redshank, ringed plover, dunlin, snipe, lapwing, six green sandpipers, two greenshank, an oystercatcher, spotted redshank and wood sandpiper. Two juvenile cuckoos and a family of yellow wagtails were seen. While I was on the Skoyles Marsh trail three grasshopper warblers were heard, and a spotted flycatcher and numerous redpolls and turtle doves all noted.

Roy and Bob arrived from Essex during the morning and we went boating. At Whiteslea we listened to a Savi's warbler, almost certainly an unattached male. En route to Rush Hills good views were had of several bearded tits. On the pool were sixty-two Canada geese, sixteen greylags, fourteen shelduck, numerous

A common snipe on its nest in a sedgebed.
per S. Linsell

mallard and teal, two drake wigeon, three little stints, three ruffs, two wood and two common sandpipers, two little ringed plover, two spotted redshank, a whimbrel and the usual dunlin, ringed plover, redshank, green sandpipers, snipe and lapwing. Also present were common and little terns, four little gulls, and yellow and pied wagtails. While we were in the hide swallowtails flew past.

Around the broad were broods of pochard, tufted duck and grebes, one carrying two young on its back. A male marsh harrier was hunting over the Big Rond.

On Swim Coots were Canadas and greylags, mallard, teal, shoveler, gadwall, a brood of shelduck, eight ruffs, two green-shank, and several snipe. On leaving the hide nine curlew flew high to the east. We then went to Whiteslea Wood, where we found lesser spotted woodpecker, tree creeper, redpolls and a blackcap.

As I drove to the Lodge this evening two cranes flew over and disappeared towards Horsey. Took a punt out round the waterways and found five singing Savi's warblers; a female marsh harrier and a bittern flew across the Sounds, where a cormorant stood on a channel post; three whimbrel flew very high southwards calling frequently, and bearded tits were vocal in many areas. Back at Whiteslea five juvenile kestrels were standing outside the nest-box where they had been born.

This was an unusually rewarding day for mid-July, a month at Hickling we normally regard as about the quietest of the year.

August is a most unpredictable month for birds; it is normally fairly rewarding, but, as the two examples show, it can in some years really turn up trumps. It should be noted that on both these dates winds were easterly.

21st August, 1977

Mainly fine, a light north-east wind, good visibility. At 0600 hours two marsh harriers flew over the marshes east of the Lodge road, putting to flight about 320 mallard. Six wheatears and several whinchats were on the Whiteslea marshes, where a juvenile red-backed shrike was on the big clump of brambles, and yellow wagtails were running around the feet of the cattle. At the Lodge a female red-backed shrike was on the overhead cables.

Approaching Chapman's pool a grasshopper warbler was reeling strongly, and on the pool were nine teal, three wood sandpipers, three green sandpipers, two ruff, and snipe, lapwing, ringed plover and a kingfisher. Moving on to Deary's pool, I found eight teal, five shoveler, eight wood sandpipers, four curlew-sandpipers, three common sandpipers, two little ringed plover, a greenshank, eleven ruff, eighteen snipe and dunlin.

Yet another five wood sandpipers were on the Observation Hut pools, along with teal, shoveler, green sandpipers, green-shank, six ruffs and two kingfishers.

The Skoyles Marsh trail produced several pied and spotted flycatchers, two wryneck, redstarts, whitethroats, lesser white-throats, blackcaps, the other regular warblers and a young cuckoo.

Took a punt to the broad pools. On Rush Hills were eighty Canada geese, 105 mallard, sixty-eight teal, thirty-two shoveler, six gadwall, three wigeon, two garganey, two little terns, one common tern, one little gull, four wood sandpipers, a broad-billed sand-piper right in front of the hide, sixteen curlew-sandpipers, one Temminck's stint, a black-tailed godwit, a golden plover, plus spotted redshanks, little stints, ruffs, a knot and all the commoner waders.

The broad was deserted by birds, being plastered with boats!

In the vicinity of Swim Coots fine views of bearded tits and a water rail, but on the pool were only fifty-seven Canadas, thirty-two mallard, four teal and two snipe. Strange there were no waders.

A rare sight this evening was a green woodpecker in the wood on Skoyles, my first sighting here. Ten curlew flew high westwards, followed later by seven oystercatchers and a black-tailed godwit. A wryneck was seen again, and a barn owl was out hunting.

All told, ninety-seven bird species were recorded today.

16th August, 1980

Mainly fine and sunny, rather hazy; a light easterly wind; very warm with a maximum of 76°F. Visibility fair.

Swim Coots is much favoured by both waders and wildfowl. S. Linsell

The early morning walk produced two cranes on a marsh near the Lodge road; whimbrel heard flying high to the south but couldn't see them; a lesser spotted woodpecker in Skoyles Wood; many hundreds of sand martins around the broad and a few swifts;

on the pools were Canada geese, mallard, teal, shoveler, gadwall, a garganey, several common, green and wood sandpipers, spotted redshanks, little stints, ruffs, greenshank, redshank, dunlin, ringed plover, snipe, lapwing, a kingfisher, and yellow and pied wagtails.

During the morning Bert and Joan Axell arrived for their annual visit. We boated round the waterways. On Rush Hills we were well rewarded with Canada geese, mallard, teal, shoveler, gadwall, a pintail, shelduck, and two tufted duck; in addition to the usual gulls there were four little gulls, as well as common, little, sandwich and arctic terns. There were twenty-three wader species, which included fourteen curlew-sandpipers, sixteen little stints, two Temminck's stints, twelve spotted redshanks, ten ruffs, seven greenshank, five wood sandpipers, plus one or two little ringed plover, golden plover, grey plover, sanderling, whimbrel and curlew. The dunlin numbered over sixty—an exceptional count.

The main waterways were very quiet, with just one or two tufted duck, pochard and grebes. Bearded tits did us proud, and near Swim Coots a Savi's warbler was heard calling. On the pool itself were some of the waders already seen, plus two black-tailed godwits.

Passerines noted on the walking trails included whitethroat, lesser whitethroat, blackcap, spotted flycatcher, redstart, a young cuckoo, and grasshopper, reed and sedge warblers.

Today ninety-three bird species were recorded.

A couple of days later a white-rumped sandpiper and a pectoral sandpiper arrived; they stayed for over a week.

Over the years September has without doubt proved the most rewarding month for birds, especially waders. Red-letter days have been many, and the following are but two examples.

6th September, 1979

A superbly warm and sunny day with the temperature reaching 74°F; wind light south-easterly; visibility crystal clear.

At 0630 hours a juvenile marsh harrier was seen to fly into Deary's pool, and when I got there it was feeding on a teal—probably a "pricked" bird that had died there. Also there were five green sandpipers, two wood sandpipers, two spotted redshank, two little ringed plover, eight ruffs, a knot, a green-shank, plus the commoner waders. Nearby was a female stonechat, rare sight these days, and a single swift flew south.

Peter Steele arrived from East Wretham during the morning, and we took a boat round the waterways. In the Sounds were the usual pochard, tufted duck, shoveler, gadwall, dabchicks and grebes, plus four wigeon and a cormorant. Then headed for Rush Hills, which was full of interest; a marsh sandpiper only thirty-five yards from the hide. Peter got busy with his sketchbook. This was our first record of this species in this country. Also present were a hundred-plus lapwing, eighty-three golden plover, five curlew-sandpiper, five spotted redshank, three Temminck's stints, six little stints, four little ringed plover, two wood sandpipers, a knot, a sanderling, and all the commoner waders. In addition, there were over 500 teal, many shoveler and gadwall, a few shelduck and wigeon, and numerous yellow and pied wagtails.

A week later Peter returned, along with Michael and Sylvia Seago, and I was able to show them a buff-breasted sandpiper and a pectoral sandpiper in addition to all the species seen on the sixth except the marsh sandpiper, which had gone. Saw a bittern in flight, and two kingfishers near the Observation Hut. Several wheatears and whinchats about the Whiteslea marshes, and along the Skoyles trail two pied flycatchers and a redstart.

12th September, 1981

Cloudy bright, a few light showers; wind light south-west; maximum temperature 68°F; visibility good.

The numerous visitors on the reserve have been well rewarded today. A notable movement of passerines, with at least a dozen blackcaps and three garden warblers just west of the house; many willow warblers and sedge warblers along the Whiteslea wall and elsewhere; three chiffchaffs were singing and numerous reed warblers near the Lodge; also seen were sand martins, white-throats, nine whinchats, four wheatears, three pied flycatchers and two spotted flycatchers, turtle doves, a redstart and two yellow wagtails flying south.

At 0715 hours a spotted crake was calling repeatedly near Chapman's west hide, and a single swift appeared. On the pools were 132 teal, fourteen gadwall, four green and two wood sandpipers, two spotted redshank, three little stints, one Temminck's stint, one curlew-sandpiper, one knot, two little ringed plover, plus redshank, greenshank, dunlin, ringed plover, snipe, lapwing, two yellow wagtails and a kingfisher.

Visitors taken to Rush Hills found the place loaded with birds: other 400 teal, thirty-three wigeon, sixteen shoveler, four gadwall, three young shelduck, a garganey, and many mallard; in addition to the waders seen on the landward pools there were no fewer than seventy-three little stints, two Temminck's stints, five curlew-sandpipers, two wood sandpipers, a pectoral sandpiper, five golden plover, two grey plover, fourteen ruffs, two spotted redshank, six knot, five common sandpipers, twenty-eight greenshank, three little ringed plover and a turnstone. While we were in the hide here a male marsh harrier flew past, and whimbrel were heard flying high to the south.

In the Sounds were many greylags and Canadas, two cormorants, four grebes, two dabchicks, and four black terns, plus two little gulls. On returning to Whiteslea a sparrowhawk and a male Montagu's harrier were seen, and a water rail was heard.

Some very satisfied customers today! Between us all 104 bird species were recorded.

October in the nineteen-eighties

Visitors to the reserve in this last month of our open season begin to tail off and finally to fade away. In a way the birds are rather the same: the summer visitors have gone and the winter visitors have not arrived in earnest. The telephone rings and someone asks, is there much to see at Hickling? And in all honesty I have to tell them that it is pretty quiet, especially on the wader pools, where visitors can visit the hides on foot. These are virtually deserted by wildfowl and waders between October and March. It appears to be a characteristic of the wildfowl family, at Hickling at any rate, that they will not spend the daylight hours where they are fed. From

The Rush Hills wader pool, where as many as forty-two pairs of little terns once nested.
S. Linsell

Three flamingoes in flight over Hickling Broad, a surprise for visiting birdwatchers. They were presumably escapees from some wildlife park or zoo.
S. Linsell

October onwards I feed Cadbury's and Chapman's pools with dross, sweepings, or whatever you like to call it, which many mallard and teal come to feed on from dusk onwards. Because there are no wildfowl on these pools by day other wintering species such as lapwing, snipe, and the occasional redshank and dunlin, appear to sense something must be wrong here and they join all the wildfowl "loafing" on the pools across the broad.

During the autumn and early winter of 1984 there was a remarkable sight on Rush Hills every time I visited it. A year earlier we had made four raised islands here, mainly as nesting sites for terns, but at this time of the year dozens of snipe "loafed" on them throughout the day. I had boarded two of the islands along the west side to prevent erosion of the soft peat by the prevailing westerly wind and waves; the boards stuck up some eight inches above the level of the islands. On many occasions on very windy days I would look out from the hide and see several snipe standing behind the boards getting some shelter from the wind. But they stood there with spray from the breaking waves soaking them, and the water running off the end of their beaks; they endured this for hours! Why did they not spend the days on the landward pools, where there was any amount of exposed mud and plenty of places to get out of the wind?

What can the visitor expect to see during this month of October? During the first half the last of the migrant swallows, house and sand martins, chiffchaffs, blackcaps, reed warblers, yellow wagtails, little stints, ruffs, and green sandpipers pass through. In most years it is the time to see ring ouzels, and it is also the time when large numbers of redwing and fieldfares are present; brambling arrive, but normally pass on and are only detected by their diagnostic calls. Immigrant blackbirds also arrive, often in considerable numbers, and there are notable movements of skylarks, meadow pipits, lapwing and wood pigeons. The first goldcrests, coal tits and water pipits arrive, the latter staying throughout the winter and often into April, when they are in glorious colour.

This is the month when there are many sightings of marsh harriers, both adults and young; wintering hen harriers, merlins and sparrowhawks arrive, and many groups of Bewick's swans pass westwards during the last week. In some years one or two rough-legged buzzards appear and may winter, and one or more spotted crakes are heard and occasionally seen. Ruffs are present in the area every winter and sometimes number up to fifty. They tend to keep on wet meadows or grazing marshes, and a few appear on the wader pools for short visits.

For the holidaymaker enjoying a late holiday on a cruiser there will be wildfowl on the main waterways: mallard, teal, shoveler, gadwall (large numbers in the Sounds), wigeon, a pintail or two, pochard, tufted duck, the first of the goldeneye, greylags and Canada geese. Keep your eyes to the Heavens during mornings, for you may be rewarded with the wonderful sight of Bewick's swans heading for the Ouse Washes against a blue sky. As you pass through Heigham Sounds keep your eyes open for great crested grebes, dabchicks, cormorants and herons; and there may be an early Slavonian or red-necked grebe. In some years one or two hooded crows put in an early appearance.

Quite often October proves to be a superbly warm and sunny month, and even if there is not a lot to see in the way of birds it is a joy to walk the pathways, or to get a boat out and find you have the waterways almost to yourself. It is a time of magnificent sunsets over a landscape turning more brown, russet and gold with the passing of each day. The lone sailor returning from downriver as the sun goes down and the wind dies away to a mere whisper frequently finds himself alone in the beautiful setting of the Sounds. If he has no inboard engine he will be forced to drop his mudweight and spend the last moments of daylight beneath a sky, and on waters, bloodred as the sun sinks below the horizon. But he will not be alone, for during the hours of darkness he will constantly hear sounds of the wild, in particular the thrilling whistles of migrating wigeon. And if the moon rides high and full, birds may be seen passing overhead on whispering wings.

Goings-on 7

THE LIFE of a warden on a busy reserve like Hickling is not all birdwatching and nest-protecting. Both come into the job, but a busy working day does not, unhappily, leave one with time for leisurely observation of the reserve's feathered population. In fact much of one's birdwatching is done, as with any other ornithologist, in what one might have regarded as one's off-duty hours.

In addition to recording the fauna and flora there is work of all kinds to be done, and parties to be escorted around the nature trails. And one thing I had to learn quickly when I arrived in 1975 from Fingringhoe Wick reserve, on the south bank of the River Colne six miles downriver from Colchester, was how to handle the 34-foot reed lighter. There was some pretty bleak weather that May as I began my course of instruction under the critical eye of Arthur Beales, a marshman all his life except for his wartime service with the Royal Navy.

We used the reed lighter to take parties on the unique water trail, which begins to operate towards the end of May. Our first party that year was from a school in the Breckland; Arthur came with me that day, and after that I was on my own.

Evening visits in those days were a rarity, though in later years I sometimes had to refuse some applications for such visits because of the increasing demand, and I most vividly remember my very first evening party. It began well enough: the sun shone warmly from a clear blue sky as I met the ladies from a certain Women's Institute near the Pleasure Boat Inn, even if the fresh easterly wind had a distinct chill in it. As we left the staithe and cruised slowly round the head of the broad, with Hill Common off our port side, I pointed out the picturesque cottages and ancient boathouses standing beside reed-fringed dykes; swallows and house martins dipped over the water or hawked for insects over the reedbeds, and a pair of swans with five cygnets preened themselves beside one of the thatched boathouses. Several common terns were diving into the water catching small fish for their mates, who were incubating eggs or brooding young on Rush Hills; a female pochard led her seven youngsters out of our path and into the safety of the reeds; and over the reeds and over the tops of the tall trees beyond them scores of swifts were revelling in a massive hatch of insects.

A short dyke little wider than our reed lighter runs up to the

Opposite page: *When the Queen opened a new conservation centre at Ranworth in 1976, the jubilee year of the Norfolk Naturalists' Trust, members of the Hickling staff were among those presented to her by Mr Timothy Colman, president of the NNT. Here the Queen chats with Arthur Beales, while Norman Belson awaits his turn.*
Eastern Daily Press

flood bank at Deary's, with our landing stage on the port side. Arriving at the head of the dyke, I ran the boat firmly in so that the bows grounded on the bottom, and we all disembarked and entered one of the nearby bird-hides. Looking out across the pool in front there was nothing really exciting to be seen, but there were five species of duck and ringed plover, redshanks, lapwings, snipe and a pair of yellow wagtails; reed and sedge warblers were singing nearby, while redpolls chattered away among the birches and sallows.

What could possibly go wrong on such an evening? We left the hide and took the short circular walk around the marsh, which is usually pretty wet; the pathway is laid on a bed of railway sleepers, so everyone's feet are kept dry. On either side was a good variety of plants: meadowsweet, hemp agrimony, flag iris, milk parsley, yellow loosestrife and many others. During the day this is a good place to see swallowtails, and in most seasons their strikingly coloured caterpillars are to be seen on the milk parsley. This evening several bearded tits appeared, to the delight of my visitors. Nobody slipped into the mud, and everybody enjoyed themselves.

Then we reached the landing stage. Our reed lighter was no longer there! To my horror I saw that the east wind had freshened while we were on the marsh, and the boat was drifting away across the broad. I had forgotten to use the mooring lines. The ladies

looked at me, and I looked at them; in particular I looked at Madam President, a rather fierce-looking lady of seventy-plus, and to her I addressed my apologies.

"Madam President", I said, "I've got to get the boat back —there's no alternative, I'll have to strip off and swim for it." Did I detect a few smiles and a twinkle in one or two eyes? But not from Madam President!

Leaving my boots and socks on the landing stage, I floundered painfully through the reedbed to the edge of the broad. There I took off my clothes and rolled them into a bundle; the reeds hid my nakedness from the ladies on the landing stage.

Holding my clothes above my head, I swam out to the reed lighter and climbed aboard. The sound of cheering and clapping reached me from ashore. Carefully putting my clothes on, I brought the boat back to the landing stage and again tendered my apologies to Madam President.

Fastening her eyes on mine, and with no trace of a smile, she said: "Mr Linsell, do you do this every time you take people on your water trail?"

There was only one other occasion when I had to make an enforced swim, and that was one February day when I had taken a boat across to Whiteslea wood; I had to break a fair bit of ice before reaching the landing stage. I left the boat securely tied up and set off on a lengthy walk to Sounds Plantation, and back via Bethel's Marshes.

This sizable area of the reserve has never been very rewarding for birds, although Sounds Plantation has had a heronry for many years. Sometimes I put up a woodcock and among the alders and birches there are usually redpolls and, rarely, siskins. It has always mystified me why this bird is so rarely seen on the reserve. There is certainly no lack of their favourite alders, yet I have had fewer than a dozen sightings over the years.

I completed my walk and arrived back on the Potter Heigham wall by Whiteslea Wood. As I headed for the landing stage a hundred yards away three youths passed me going in the opposite direction. When I reached the staging I saw my boat was no longer there: it had been cast adrift and pushed several yards along the channel I had cleared of ice, and the fresh wind was taking it steadily further away. The three youths were obviously the culprits, and I sprinted after them silently on the grassy turf. When I was about the length of a cricket pitch from them one of them glanced behind him and saw me coming, and they raced along the wall with me yelling curses after them. Alas, youth was on their side and they outpaced me.

123

Back at the landing stage I decided there were only two options open to me. I could either walk home, about six miles, or I could strip off and swim for the boat. Although it was a very cold day I chose the latter, and fifteen minutes later was thawing out in a hot bath with a hot whisky in my hand.

Several amusing incidents have occurred on the water trail; I remember three in particular. One morning I was on the tree tower with the visitors I was escorting, including a lady of nearly eighty. She said she was not going to be the only one unable to climb the sixty feet of ladders, but when it was time to leave the tower she wasn't looking forward to the descent. As she slowly moved down the first ladder one of the men still on the top with me turned to me and in deadly seriousness said, "I work for the London Fire Service. I'm sure if you wrote to my Chief and explained what you have here, and the problems you experience, I'm sure you would get a canvas fire-escape shute which people could jump into and whizz to the ground!" What a splendid idea, but I didn't follow it up.

On another occasion we had all come down from the tree tower and I was leading the way out of the wood back to the boat. Bringing up the rear of the party was a youngish married couple. Nobody happened to be talking at the time and all was very peaceful when the wife said to her husband in a whisper which I'm sure she did not intend the rest of the party to hear, "Thought you said you couldn't climb ladders!" I assume he had to do the decorating from then on.

One morning as we left the wood I locked the gate after me and followed my visitors down to the boat. It was only just as I was casting off that a very jovial man exclaimed loudly "You won't go without the wife, will you?"

A rapid head count revealed that I was one short. "Where on earth is she?" I asked. "You've locked her in the wood—she went to spend a penny."

"Well, that's one way of getting rid of her," commented some wag in the boat.

That was one of the jolliest parties I ever took around the reserve. Not all our visitors are so jolly, or so well behaved. I particularly remember a Saturday afternoon during that blistering summer of 1976 when I was escorting a party on what I always called the dedicated birdwatchers' boat tour, a rather pleasant and somewhat exclusive tour but very time-consuming as far as the warden was concerned. We had made our calls at the hides at Rush Hills North and Swim Coots and were on our way to Rush Hills South hide when a movement there caught my eye.

Roy King, director of Abberton Reservoir wildfowl ringing station, and Bob Gardiner on the "dedicated birdwatchers' boat tour" of Hickling.
S. Linsell

Through my binoculars I saw the masts of two boats; five people were peering over the tops of the reed screens, causing all the birds on the pool to take to the wing, while two others were trying to break into the locked hide. When we arrived at the landing stage, which was blocked by their two sailing dinghies, they took not the slightest notice of my shouts. It was only when I threatened to tow their boats away that one of the party, a military-looking man in navy blazer, grey flannels and collar and tie, turned round and said in an Oxford accent, "Don't worry, old boy, we're all RSPB members." Words did not fail me!

Then there were the "visitors" we had one morning during the nesting season of 1977. The morning of Sunday, 29th May, was fine, with hardly a breath of wind, and at six o'clock I was pushing a punt from Whiteslea to Rush Hills. Sedge and reed warblers were chattering away, and bearded tits "pinged" as I silently passed near them. By the entrance to the dyke a female pochard slipped off her nest, where she was incubating six eggs. The main purpose of visiting the Rush Hills hide was to check on the nesting little terns. Against the dark muddy background every bird could be seen without the aid of binoculars, even those at the further of the two colonies a hundred yards away. The other colony was only a few yards in front of the hide. I noted that all birds were sitting where they should be, and there were quite a few pairs not yet settled down and nesting.

I then searched the slad to see what else was about, and as I slowly swung my binoculars from right to left four men suddenly leapt into view as they emerged from the fringe of reeds on the far side. All had haversacks on their backs. My immediate reaction was that they were egg collectors.

Rush Hills, fortunately, is surrounded by water. On the north, west and south sides lies the broad, while through the reedbed along its eastern side runs a broad dyke preventing access on to Rush Hills from the flood bank, a public footpath. And it was impossible for them to walk from where they were to the tern colonies, for running from east to west across the middle of the slad is a relict dyke, long since filled in with liquid mud, leading at both ends into existing dykes. It is a highly dangerous place, and impassable.

Knowing that the terns' eggs were safe, I decided to ignore the men for the moment and to find out how they had managed to gain

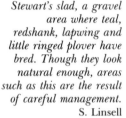

Stewart's slad, a gravel area where teal, redshank, lapwing and little ringed plover have bred. Though they look natural enough, areas such as this are the result of careful management.
S. Linsell

access. So I got back into the punt and pushed myself with all speed towards Deep Dyke and then into the dyke running through the reedbed. As I rounded the one bend in this long dyke I saw stretched across it in the distance a plank, what Norfolk marshmen call a "ligger". As I drew near to it I crouched low; I didn't want the four men, somewhere off to my right, to see me.

I glided silently to the ligger and slowly stood upright, peering across the reedtops left and right, but saw nobody. Then I looked at the ligger; it consisted of two stout boards, each about ten feet long and over two inches thick, bolted end to end, with aluminium carrying handles at each end. A very portable bridge indeed! No ordinary birdwatchers these, I reflected, for they had carried their bridge well over a mile from the nearest road. I had no doubt that these were professional egg collectors.

I quietly eased the ligger into the dyke and secured it to a line on the punt. There followed a long, slow push back to Whiteslea, where I climbed to the lookout and searched in vain for a sight of the four men. They were somewhere within the reedbed, concealed by the tall reeds.

It was time for breakfast; I had visitors to take on a boat tour at ten o'clock—that would include a visit to Rush Hills. When we arrived there two of the men could be seen struggling through the reedbed towards Deep Dyke; but of the other two there was no sign. At half past twelve I was back on the lookout and could see all four men on the south bank of Deep Dyke, thumbing a lift from passing boats. I got back into my boat, removed the warden's flag, and headed for them. As I got near one of them called: "Can you give us a lift?" I cut the motor and shouted back: "Where's your boat? You can only get here by boat." Another replied: "We haven't got a boat. We crossed a bridge somewhere over there and somebody's removed it. We're stranded." I walked forward to the bows and replaced my flag. Their faces visibly dropped. "I removed it," I said. "That will teach you to come here and take birds' eggs. Hope you get a lift". And I returned home for lunch.

I had more visitors to take out in the afternoon, and on my return to Whiteslea at half past four I climbed to the lookout again. All four of them were still on the bank in Deep Dyke and still trying to get a lift. I went and paid them another visit. "What!," I said, "still here? Never mind, patience is a virtue." And I went home for tea; it was almost nine hours since I had removed that ligger.

As is my custom I take our two dogs for a walk after supper when the evenings are long, and on this evening I couldn't resist returning to the lookout. All four were still there. I never did discover how they got off, if indeed they did.

A few days later when I was in the village an old marshman came up to me with a broad smile and said: "Heard about them ole egg thieves you had. I reckons I knows where them are. Go you down Rush Hills again and push the quant in that dyke, not against the bank. I reckons that's where them bodies are!" A few days later I returned to that dyke and did as he had suggested. My quant sank into about five feet of treacherous liquid mud. There were no bodies there, but I've never had any further visits from egg thieves.

One autumn night I was out in my punt on the wide and beautiful expanse of Heigham Sounds, when I saw the brilliant light from a gas lantern in a boat occupied by anglers, fishing for bream most likely. They were some distance ahead, their small rowing boat tucked into the fringe of reeds. Through my night-glasses I could see them quite clearly, but could not recognize them. I kept to the middle of the channel so as not to disturb their sport. There was the quiet murmur of conversation as I passed silently and unseen. Or so I thought.

Suddenly there came a hoarse cry: "Jack, look! There's someone walking on the bleedin' water!" A brief pause, then: "Bloody Hell!" followed by utter silence.

I gave a push with the quant and altered course towards them, trying desperately not to burst into laughter. Instead I called out: "Don't worry, gentlemen, I'm not Jesus Christ, only the old warden." It transpired that the combination of their blinding gas-light and the brilliant full moon had made only the top half of me faintly visible to them. We had a right old laugh about that.

The hot summer of 1976 posed its problems for us at Hickling, for by August everything was tinder dry and my greatest fear was a fire on the reserve. It needed only a cigarette end thrown into the sun-baked vegetation to start a fire that could travel for miles, even jumping across the dykes in such conditions.

One blisteringly hot Saturday afternoon that August I was taking four ladies on the dedicated birdwatchers' tour when I was stunned to see smoke rising from Turner's Island. Some lunatic, I thought, has started a fire! I explained to my party that we must make a diversion from our normal route to investigate.

As we rounded the corner of a reedbed and the island came into full view I put my binoculars to my eyes—and nearly fell overboard. There was a man up one of the willows sawing off dead branches and dropping them to someone else who was stoking a fire.

I glanced down into the boat, saw the large bailer lying under one of the seats, and inspiration came to me. Leaning over the side

Two members of the reserve staff, Arthur Beales and Norman Belson, renewing reed screens at the approach to one of the bird-hides. Such tasks keep them busy throughout the year.
S. Linsell

I filled the bailer with water and handed it to one of my passengers to hold.

Revving the engine, we roared towards the island. As we grounded I grabbed the bailer, leapt off the bows and ran towards the group of people round the fire, shouting at the top of my voice "Don't panic, I'll help you put it out!" They just stood there, dad, mum and the children, staring at me as though I had gone stark raving mad.

The shallow water in the broad got almost hot that summer, to the delight of the algae, which multiplied at a tremendous rate, turning the water into what looked like condensed pea soup. The propeller of every boat churned up the mud, making the water even more turbid. There was no hope of the continuous sunshine reaching any aquatic plants that might have existed on the bottom of the broad.

In the vicinity of the Pleasure Boat Inn the state of the water was even worse, for added to the pea soup and mud slurry was diesel oil and much sundry litter. Many years ago the boatyards instructed holidaymakers to remember to pump out the bilges every morning; I can only think that this clearing of the bilges was responsible for the covering of oil in the vicinity of the staithe.

Picture if you can this foul mixture trapped in the dyke leading to the inn. You will never see any of the local people paddling in it, let alone swimming in it, these days.

Imagine our surprise one August day when we returned to the dyke at the conclusion of our water trail to find a number of people swimming in all this filth. "You must be out of your minds swimming in this!" I called out to them.

Back came the reply in a guttural accent: "This is vunderfull, you should see our Rhine!"

Holidaymakers in yachts and motor cruisers often get themselves into trouble. There was the German family who were enjoying their holiday in a sailing cruiser until they gybed just as the boat was passing too close to one of the posts marking the channel across Hickling Broad. The mainsheet wrapped itself round the post and in a flash the boat was laid on its side, the mast hitting the water with a mighty smack. This family knew their stuff, however. Father dashed forward to lower the sail as the boat righted itself, and

As the boat's bows passed under the bridge there was a mighty crash . . .
P. Steele

when I came alongside to offer help they said no, they knew what had to be done.

Then there was a French couple on a cycling tour who hired a rowing boat from the staithe and set off to see Hickling Broad. It was a fine sunny day with an abundance of high cumulus clouds, which usually means the wind is going to get stronger and stronger until evening, when it dies away to no more than a whisper. So it was that, having crossed the broad before a moderate west wind, when they turned to row back they could make no progress, and it was not long before the oarsman became exhausted and the boat was blown into the reeds. How grateful they were for a tow back to the staithe behind the warden's boat.

Another mishap that could have had disastrous consequences occurred when a large old sailing cruiser with a long bowsprit, manned by a crew somewhat lacking in experience, was tacking along Deep Dyke towards the broad against a strong westerly wind. The girl at the helm misjudged the distance between her boat and a cruiser moored on the south bank, with the result that the bowsprit burst through the side of the moored boat. There's never a dull moment on Hickling!

My first insight into what can go on in these parts came when we were on holiday in 1955, and our sons said they wanted to go to watch the big boats going under the bridge at Potter Heigham. Several boats passed through the bridge without incident as we sat on the bank about seventy yards downstream from the old brick bridge. The boys were greatly disappointed; they became bored and went off to the shops with mother. While they were away a large cruiser with a collapsible canopy over the steering position came upriver past the large notices which declared "Dead Slow—Lower Your Canopy". The cruiser did not slacken speed, and warning yells were answered only with a cheery wave.

As the boat's bows passed under the bridge there was a mighty crash, mahogany and glass flew in all directions, and the boat shuddered to a halt. It was just being moored on the opposite bank when another boat attempted to pass under the bridge with its canopy up, with the same result.

My two sons flatly refused to believe me when told what had happened while they were away shopping. They did return in time to see the sailing dinghy with a young lad at the helm obviously intent on sailing under the bridge.

Regretfully I did not witness the "goings-on" on Hickling Broad in the summer of 1985, but I heard all about them from those who did.

For as long as local people can remember Little Pleasure

Island was made visible in the middle of the broad by the reeds which grew on its submerged hard clay and gravel base. During the early eighties the rapidly increasing population of Canada and greylag geese found the new growth of reed on the island, and elsewhere, very tempting, and within four years the reeds on Little Pleasure Island had all been grazed away.

One Saturday afternoon a catamaran was being sailed across the broad by a man and a woman who were evidently unaware of the existence of the now-invisible island just six inches or so below the surface. One of those who was watching told me later that the catamaran stopped dead when it hit the island, and the crew were catapulted into the broad.

I marked the extremities of the island with stakes soon after that incident.

A Fishing Interlude 8

I AM indebted to the Editor of *Shooting Times and Country Magazine* for allowing me to quote extracts from an article by D. D. Pye published on 17th September, 1967, when all was still well with the Broads and fishing was a joy.

Norfolk Broads—Mecca of Coarse Fishing

Norfolk, with its two hundred miles of rivers and well over two thousand acres of Broads, is to my mind the Mecca of coarse fishing.

From Hickling Broad and its surrounding waters, I have taken 253 pike of 20lb and over since 1952. One might think that I only fish for pike, but I can assure readers that I fish mostly for other species. It was just after the war when I started fishing for pike in earnest. It all started with a conversation I had with a great friend of mine who is a game warden on Hickling Broad. He told me of the devastation caused to the fish stocks by the tremendous flood of 1938, when the sea broke through the defences on to Horsey Mere. What impressed me most was the size of the dead pike he had seen floating on the surface.

Up to this time I had caught many pike but never one of 20lb. I made up my mind that I would catch some of these big pike. Only a few years had passed and the waters in the area had already recovered from the devastating salt water. This was proved by the fact that the headkeeper, the late Jim Vincent, now a legendary name among pike anglers, was catching big pike from Hickling. Although Jim Vincent never enjoyed the success I have had with pike, his record will stand for many years among the spinning enthusiasts, for that was his only method of pike fishing. His total was 29 fish of 20lb and over, the heaviest being 29lb 8oz.

Knowing Hickling as I do, I marvel at the way he spun his large spoon through the shallow heavily-weeded water. Needless to say, the Vincent spoon is named after him.

Hickling is Norfolk's biggest broad; it covers some 460 acres with an average depth of about 4 feet, and is gin-clear. In the hot summer months, the rudd fishing on Hickling Broad and Horsey Mere can be wonderful; very early morning and late evening these plump golden-bodied fish can be heard as well as seen, breaking the smooth surface of the water. It is at these times when a floating

crust will almost surely be the best bait to catch them. I use a 12-foot built cane rod, fixed spool reel loaded with 4lb b.s.l. and a No 6 hook, a porcupine float and one swanshot. The hook is placed about two feet from the float, which has the shot right up tight beneath it. These are used only as weight for casting. The whole of the line is greased, including the length from float to hook. I use a piece of crust about the size of a half-crown. Never cast the tackle right among the playing fish, but to the side in order to avoid scaring them. Almost immediately one will see the movement of the rudd moving towards the floating bait. A big swirl and the bait and float will shoot along the surface; a firm deliberate strike will hook the fish. Once hooked it must be taken away from the shoal as quickly as possible. For about two seconds after a fish is hooked it is taken completely by surprise; it is in this time that the angler should move the hooked fish a couple of yards away from the others.

On windless days or on bays that are protected from the wind, rudd may be seen throughout the day, swimming just below the surface. Depth or weed-growth matters little to this species. They swim and play among the reeds and weeds, sometimes showing the tips of their dorsal fins above the surface. When fishing for rudd under these conditions I prefer paste for bait. My tackle is just the same, the only difference being the distance between hook and float, which is never *more* than ten inches, often less.

I row my boat quietly round the edges of the broad, stopping to watch for fish movement in the bays and inlets that can be found on all of the broads in this area, though some are not visible as bays at first glance. One may see what appears to be a thinning of the reeds. A further search will reveal a small bay hidden behind them. It is in such places that the rudd will swim during the day away from the ever-moving holiday craft. When fish are found playing in such places the angler should keep down and make long casts using knobs of paste the size of a shilling. Sometimes a good number of fish can be taken in quick succession; at other times the shoal will vanish completely after two or three have been caught; it is then best to move on to the next spot. One thing should be remembered. To avoid unnecessary damage and suffering to the fish, always empty the keep-net before moving off; strange as it may seem, towing fish in a keep-net drowns them.

The tench fishing is also good on Hickling and dykes that join in to the main Thurne. In fact, all the upper reaches of the River Thurne hold a good head of these splendid fish. The best time to fish for them is early and late in the day. Paste is my favourite bait, but small red worms and maggots are also good. The reason I do not use the latter is that they will take perch and eels which are also plentiful in the area, and one of these hooked in a good tench swim does not improve sport among tench.

I would advise a visitor to the area to first make a recce of the fishing spots. The thing to look for is the gravel-bottomed channels around the edges of the broad; usually about four feet in depth, they are the haunts of tench. I keep about twenty yards out and cast my baits close to the reeds, using a laying-on technique. The tackle is the same as for rudd fishing, the only difference being the distance from float to shot. When fishing a swim 4 feet deep I place my shot about five feet from the float; by taking in a little line, the float will lie at half-cock.

The average size of the tench on these waters is around 4lb, but I have taken more above. In fact, I believe I hold the actual Broads record with a fish of 6½ lb. My only hope is that one day I might hook and boat the pike that will break the English record of 37½ lb, but whether such a fish falls to my rod or to that of any other angler, it will take some catching.

Notes and References

Chapter one

1 R. Malster. *Wherries and Waterways.*
2 E. A. Ellis. *The Broads*, p. 110.
3 *Eastern Daily Press*, 6 October, 1933.

Chapter two

1 J. M. Lambert. "The past, present and future of the Norfolk Broads".
2 J. M. Lambert et al. *The Making of the Broads.*
3 J. W. Gregory. "The physical features of the Norfolk Broads".
4 W. A. Dutt. *The Norfolk Broads*, p. 12.
5 Ibid., pp. 10–12.
6 Anthony Buxton. *Fisherman Naturalist*, pp. 106–108.
7 E. Hosking. *An Eye for a Bird*, p. 108.
8 G. Yates. *Bird Haunts in Southern England*, p. 20.
9 E. Vincent. *A Season of Birds*, pp. 18–20.
10 C. McLean. *At Dawn and Dusk*, p. 67.
11 Ibid., pp. 40–41.
12 *Eastern Daily Press.*

Chapter three

1 Aubrey Buxton. *The King in his Country*, p. 103.
2 C. McLean. *At Dawn and Dusk*, p. 46.

Chapter four

1 E. L. Turner. Article in *The Romance of Nature*, p. 1284.

Chapter five

1 R. Lubbock. *The Fauna of Norfolk*, 1845.
2 R. Lubbock. *The Fauna of Norfolk*, 1879.
3 E. Vincent. *A Season of Birds*, pp. 81–83.
4 E. L. Turner. *Broadland Birds*, pp. 3–4.
5 M. Seago. *Birds of Norfolk.*
6 Lord William Percy. "The Bittern".
7 E. L. Turner. *Broadland Birds*, pp. 9–10.
8 Ibid., pp. 15–22.
9 Lubbock, 1879.
10 H. Stevenson. *The Birds of Norfolk*, p. 152.
11 B. B. Riviere. *A History of the Birds of Norfolk*, pp. 48–50.
12 E. L. Turner. *Broadland Birds*, p. 16.
13 M. Seago. *Birds of Norfolk.*

14   Lubbock, 1845, p. 122.
15   Lubbock, 1879, p. 170.
16   H. Stevenson, quoted in Lubbock, 1879, pp. 168–169.
17   Lubbock, 1845, p. 14.
18   J. Vincent. "The marsh and hen-harriers", in *The Romance of Nature*, pp. 1315–1319.
19   J. Vincent. "The Montagu's harrier", in *The Romance of Nature*, p. 1186.

Bibliography

Anon, ed. *The Romance of Nature.* Country Life, n.d.

Buxton, Anthony. *Fisherman Naturalist.* Collins, 1946.

Buxton, Aubrey. *The King in his Country.* Longmans, Green, 1955.

Dutt, W. A. *The Norfolk Broads.* Methuen, 1903, 1905 and 1930.

Ellis, E. A. *The Broads.* Collins, 1965.

Emerson, P. H. *Birds, Beasts and Fishes of the Norfolk Broadland.* David Nutt, 1895.

Hosking, E. *An Eye for a Bird.* Hutchinson, 1970.

Lambert, J. M., Jennings, J. N., Smith, C. T., Green, Charles, and Hutchinson, J. N. *The Making of the Broads.* Royal Geographical Society, 1960.

Lubbock, R. *Observations on the Fauna of Norfolk, and more particularly on The District of the Broads.* Norwich: Charles Muskett, 1845; second edition, Norwich: Henry W. Stacy, 1858; new edition with additions from unpublished manuscripts of the author and notes by Thomas Southwell, Norwich: Jarrold and Sons, 1879.

McLean, C. *At Dawn and Dusk.* Batchworth Press, 1954.

Malster, R. *Wherries and Waterways.* Terence Dalton, 1971, 1986.

Riviere, B. B. *A History of the Birds of Norfolk.* H. F. & G. Witherby, 1930.

Rye, W. *The Hickling Broad Case Micklethwait v. Vincent: The Judgment of the Court of Appeal Considered.* Norwich: Agas H. Goose, 1893.

Seago, M. *Birds of Norfolk.* Norwich: Jarrold and Sons, 1967, 1977.

Stevenson, H. *The Birds of Norfolk.* Vol. I, London: John van Voorst; Norwich: Matchett and Stevenson, 1866; vol. II, London: John van Voorst; Norwich: Stevenson and Co., 1870; vol. III, London: Gurney and Jackson; Norwich: Norfolk Chronicle Co. Ltd, 1890.

Turner, E. L. *Broadland Birds*. Country Life, 1924.

Vincent, E. *A Season of Birds: A Norfolk Diary, 1911*. Weidenfeld and Nicolson, 1980.

Wentworth Day, J. *Broadland Adventure*. Country Life, 1951.

Wentworth Day, J. *The Most English Corner of All England*

Yates, G. *Bird Haunts in Southern England*. Faber & Faber, 1947.

Articles

Gregory, J. W. "The physical features of the Norfolk Broads", *Natural Science*, vol. I, 1892.

Lambert, J. M. "The past, present and future of the Norfolk Broads", *Transactions of the Norfolk and Norwich Naturalists' Society*, vol. XVII, 1953.

Percy, Lord William. "The Bittern", *Country Life*, 1937.

Pye, D. "Norfolk Broads – Mecca of coarse fishing", *Shooting Times*, 17 September, 1967.

Vincent, J. "The Montagu's harrier", *Country Life*, 1936.

Vincent, J. "The marsh harrier", *Country Life*, 1937.

Original sources

Vincent, J. Personal diaries, 1911–1944.

Appendix one

A Checklist of the Birds of Hickling Reserve, 1911–1987

Black-throated diver *Gavia arctica.* Recorded almost annually up to 1944, none recorded since.

Great Northern diver *Gavia immer.* Five records up to 1944, none since.

Red-throated diver *Gavia stellata.* Recorded annually up to 1944; now a scarce winter visitor. Four 29th August, 1985.

Great crested grebe *Podiceps cristatus.* Resident, up to ten breeding pairs annually.

Red-necked grebe *Podiceps grisegena.* One or more recorded in winter most years.

Slavonian grebe *Podiceps auritus.* One or more recorded in winter most years; one 15th May, 1981.

Black-necked grebe *Podiceps nigricollis.* Rare winter visitor; one 23rd June, 1987.

Little grebe *Tachybaptus ruficollis.* Numerous between autumn and early spring; one pair bred successfully 1984–1987.

Fulmar *Fulmarus glacialis.* One 8th June, 1980; one 11th June, 1986.

Manx shearwater *Puffinus puffinus.* One 30th August, 1960.

Cormorant *Phalacrocorax carbo.* Present all year, up to twenty-four in winter. Adults of continental race *sinensis*, number up to five, February to April.

Shag *Phalacrocorax aristotelis.* One or two present most winters.

Grey heron *Ardea cinerea.* Resident; up to twenty breeding pairs in nineteen-seventies, had declined to thirteen pairs in 1987.

Purple heron *Ardea purpurea.* Four records prior to 1944; one 4th–6th May, 1979, 14th June, 1983, 8th–9th June and 30th July, 1985, 24th July, 1987.

Little egret *Egretta garzetta.* One 29th May, 1981, 25th May, 1985.

Cattle egret *Bubulcus ibis.* One 10th July, 1974, 14th to 24th April, 1975, two 26th–27th September, 1986.

Squacco heron *Ardeola ralloides.* One in July, 1912; one 22nd–27th July, 1942.

Great white heron *Egretta alba.* One 10th–18th August, 1979, 15th July, 1985.

Night heron *Nycticorax nycticorax.* One 28th October, 1974, 4th September, 1982.

Little bittern *Ixobrychus minutus.* Three records of single birds up to 1944. One 20th September, 1952.

Bittern *Botaurus stellaris.* Formerly numerous resident; only one male in early nineteen-eighties, now probably no longer breeds; few in winter.

White stork *Ciconia ciconia.* One 19th May, 1915, 8th–9th September, 1982, two 11th–12th April, 1984.

139

Spoonbill *Platalea leucorodia.* Recorded almost annually since 1911; less numerous now than in nineteen-seventies, when up to twelve present.

Glossy ibis *Plegadis falcinellus.* One 14th September, 1926, 12th November, 1943, six 25th–26th October, 1945, one 29th May, 1981.

Flamingo *Phoenicopterus ruber.* Four, probably "escapes", 26th June, 1977.

Mallard *Anas platyrhynchos.* Common resident; up to 1,400 present in autumn and up to 500 in winter.

Teal *Anas crecca crecca.* Resident; a few breeding pairs. Peak autumn count of 2,027 October, 1982; up to 1,000 in winter.

Green-winged teal *Anas crecca carolinensis.* A drake 21st–25th April, 1980, 3rd December, 1981.

Blue-winged teal *Anas discors.* A duck shot 27th September, 1975, just outside reserve boundary.

Garganey *Anas querquedula.* Less numerous and regular now on passage spring and autumn; occasionally breeds.

Gadwall *Anas strepera.* Breeding population increased since the nineteen-seventies to about twenty pairs. Autumn peak count of 254 October, 1983.

Wigeon *Anas penelope.* Formerly scarce breeder; one or two remain in summer. Winter maximum up to 1,200.

American wigeon *Anas americana.* A drake 15th September, 1931—first Norfolk record.

Pintail *Anas acuta.* Recorded in all months, one to three in summer and winter; peak counts of sixteen in January, 1980, sixteen in March, 1985.

Shoveler *Anas clypeata.* Up to twenty breeding pairs. Peak winter count of 136 in September, 1987.

Red-crested pochard *Netta rufina.* One 29th March, 1911, 5th May, 1951, 22nd April to 20th May, 1954, one shot 7th January, 1961.

Scaup *Aythya marila.* Formerly a regular winter visitor, now very scarce. One 20th December, 1975, 22nd January, 1984.

Tufted duck *Aythya fuligula.* First Broadland breeding pair, 1912. Resident; up to six pairs breed; peak winter count of 336 November, 1986.

Pochard *Aythya ferina.* Resident, up to ten breeding pairs. Winter flocks of hundreds prior to 1960, now maximum 200, but 328 on 16th February, 1986.

Ferruginous duck *Aythya nyroca.* Fourteen records up to 1930. One 2nd December, 1938, 3rd January, 1940.

Goldeneye *Bucephala clangula.* Winter visitor, less numerous than in past. Peak count of fifty-eight in February, 1984. A drake in July, 1985.

(Buffle-headed goldeneye *Bucephala albeda.* A pair 11th February, 1913, from J. Vincent diary.)

Long-tailed duck *Clangula hyemalis.* Rare; one 29th December, 1931, 4th December, 1937, 13th November, 1976, 1st–19th December, 1985.

Common scoter *Melanitta nigra.* Formerly regular winter visitor, now rare.

Velvet scoter *Melanitta fusca.* Many records up to 1934, none since.

Ruddy duck *Oxyura jamaicensis.* Rare winter visitor since 1981.

Red-breasted merganser *Mergus serrator.* Scarce winter visitor. Peak count of eighteen on 3rd March, 1979.

Goosander *Mergus merganser.* Scarce winter visitor. Peak counts of sixty on 10th February, 1924, twenty-five on 25th February, 1940, twenty-two on 12th January, 1941, sixteen on 15th February, 1987.

Smew *Mergus albellus.* Regular late winter visitor. Peak count of fourteen on 13th March, 1987.

Shelduck *Tadorna tadorna.* About five pairs breed annually, up to thirty present in spring.

Ruddy shelduck *Tadorna ferruginea.* Two present for two weeks in November, 1915.

Egyptian goose *Alopochen aegyptiacus.* Up to six occasionally seen in winter; twelve on 21st November, 1986.

Greylag goose *Anser anser.* Resident since 1978. Fourteen pairs bred in 1987. Peak count of 247 in October, 1987.

White-fronted goose *Anser albifrons albifrons.* Regular winter visitor, normally about forty but 240 on 6th February, 1984. A pair ("escapes") nested successfully 1985 and 1986.

Bean goose *Anser fabalis.* Three records up to 1944. Five 16th February, 1979, several skeins passed south-west 2nd to 4th December, 1982.

Pink-footed goose *Anser brachyrhynchus.* Small numbers most winters, but eighty on 8th February, 1984, eighty-eight on 20th December, 1987.

Brent goose *Branta bernicla bernicla.* Six 2nd April, 1976, two 6th April, 1977, one 28th April to 3rd May, 1983.

Barnacle goose *Branta leucopsis.* An irregular winter visitor. Fifteen present 26th January to 2nd February, 1984.

Canada goose *Branta canadensis.* Resident, about fifteen breeding pairs. Peak count of 236 in October, 1984, but few in winter.

Lesser snow goose *Anser coerulescens coerulescens.* One blue phase adult with 142 Bewick's swans 2nd to 4th March, 1981; possibly an "escape".

Mute swan *Cygnus olor.* Up to 1968 resident population numbered about 400, mostly non-breeders. Only three breeding pairs 1987, and up to forty non-breeders.

Whooper swan *Cygnus cygnus.* Regular winter visitor. Peak count of 102 on 1st January, 1978.

Bewick's swan *Cygnus bewickii.* Winter visitor, regular on passage autumn and early spring. Peak counts of 166 on 12th February, 1982, 202 on 17th January, 1986.

Buzzard *Buteo buteo.* One, sometimes two, usually spring and late summer.

Rough-legged buzzard *Buteo lagopus.* Recorded most winters, maximum three. One 25th June, 1975, 21st April, 1986.

Sparrowhawk *Accipter nisus.* One pair probably breeds locally. Up to four prey on starling roosts.

Goshawk *Accipter gentilis.* One 25th November, 1942, 17th November, 1979, 8th November, 1981, 12th January, 1982, 28th October, 1986.

Red Kite *Milvus milvus.* One 11th April, 1976, 10th June, 1983, 14th March, 1987.

Black Kite *Milvus migrans.* One 30th January to 21st February, 1980, one 30th–31st January and 14th–21st February, 1981.

White-tailed eagle *Haliaeëtus albicilla.* Seven records up to 1941. One 17th May, 1984.

Marsh harrier *Circus aeruginosus.* One to three pairs bred regularly up to 1959, then one or two pairs 1976 to 1978, two pairs 1985 and 1987. One or two usually winter.

Hen harrier *Circus cyaneus.* Quite numerous autumn to spring.

Montagu's harrier *Circus pygargus*. Former breeding species up to 1956. Now irregular on passage late spring and early autumn.

Osprey *Pandion haliaetus*. Regular passage migrant until early nineteen-seventies, now scarce due to lack of fish. Two 23rd May, 1985.

Hobby *Falco subbuteo*. One or two recorded most years August–September; a pair all summer 1982 and 1986.

Peregrine *Falco peregrinus*. Rare winter visitor.

Merlin *Falco columbarius*. One or two annually October to March.

Red-footed falcon *Falco vespertinus*. Several records up to 1944. A male 16th May, 1984, 28th–30th May, 1987.

Kestrel *Falco tinnunculus*. Resident, two or three breeding pairs.

Red-legged partridge *Alectoris rufa*. Resident, one or two pairs breed.

Partridge *Perdix perdix*. Now a very scarce resident.

Quail *Coturnix coturnix*. A nest with eggs, 1923; a pair bred just outside reserve 1983; one 6th September, 1985.

Pheasant *Phasianus colchicus*. Common resident.

Crane *Grus grus*. Up to six regularly seen since 1978.

Water rail *Rallus aquaticus*. Numerous resident up to 1982, since when severe winters have greatly reduced numbers.

Spotted crake *Porzana porzana*. Former breeding species, now one or two in winter only.

Little crake *Porzana parva*. One 11th April, 1924, 18th April, 1932.

Corncrake *Crex crex*. Eleven records up to 1944.

Moorhen *Gallinula chloropus*. Common resident.

Coot *Fulica atra*. Common resident. Huge winter population up to mid nineteen-sixties, now peak counts of about 200.

Purple gallinule *Porphyrio porphyrio*. One in March, 1913, and June, 1914; one in July, 1968, and May, 1975.

Oystercatcher *Haematopus ostralegus*. One pair has nested annually since 1979. Occasionally up to ten present.

Lapwing *Vanellus vanellus*. Resident, up to sixteen pairs breed. Many continental immigrants arrive late May onwards.

Ringed plover *Charadrius hiaticula hiaticula*. Up to seven pairs breed annually. Many migrants in spring and autumn, scarce in winter.

Little ringed plover *Charadrius dubius*. Recorded in 1914 and 1920. Regular spring and autumn migrant. One pair nested 1984, but eggs deserted.

Kentish plover *Charadrius alexandrinus*. One or two recorded in spring most years. One pair attempted nesting 1978.

Grey plover *Pluvialis aquatorola*. Occurs regularly in small numbers spring and autumn.

Golden plover *Pluvialis apricaria*. Winter visitor; hundreds pass through in August and September.

Turnstone *Arenaria interpres*. Small numbers occur on passage spring and autumn.

Snipe *Gallinago gallinago*. Resident; up to sixteen pairs breed. Autumn influxes of 300 or more in some years; few in winter.

Great snipe *Gallinago media*. Seven records up to 1944. One 24th May, 1978, 26th May and 17th September, 1986.

A ringed plover at Hickling, May, 1970. These birds breed on some of the wader pools.
G. St J. Hollis

Jack snipe *Lymnocryptes minimus.* Two or three recorded annually September to April.

Woodcock *Scolopax rusticola.* One or two resident pairs. Many birds from the Continent in winter.

Curlew *Numenius arquata.* Recorded in most months, strong westward passage late June to August.

Whimbrel *Numenius phaeopus.* Small numbers on spring and autumn migrations, most numerous in August.

Black-tailed godwit *Limosa limosa.* One pair nested 1934. Occurs on passage in small numbers spring and autumn.

Bar-tailed godwit *Limosa lapponica.* Variable numbers occur annually in spring and autumn.

Green sandpiper *Tringa ochropus.* A few occur on passage in spring; often twenty or more in August; one or two occasionally winter.

Wood sandpiper *Tringa glareola.* One or two observed in late spring; up to sixteen on passage in August, few in September.

Common sandpiper *Tringa hypoleucos.* A few on passage in spring; many between July and early October, peak counts of thirty in August.

Solitary sandpiper *Tringa solitaria.* One 1st to 2nd August, 1942.

Redshank *Tringa totanus.* About twelve breeding pairs; many migrants pass through in August and September; scarce in winter.

Spotted redshank *Tringa erythropus.* Regular on passage in spring and autumn, most numerous in August.

Lesser yellowlegs *Tringa flavipes.* One 24th–27th June, 1985.

Greenshank *Tringa nebularia.* Observed from April to October, most numerous in August–September, when up to twenty present.

Marsh sandpiper *Tringa stagnatilis.* One 5th June, 1925, 6th September, 1979.

Long-billed dowitcher *Limnodromus scolopaceus*. Two 19th September, 1981, 24th to 25th October, 1983.

Knot *Calidris canatus*. Small numbers on spring and autumn passage.

Purple sandpiper *Calidris maritima*. Four records up to 1944. One 27th August, 1980, 22nd January, 1983, 13th to 15th February, 1986.

Little stint *Calidris minuta*. A few on spring migration, often very numerous in autumn, when up to seventy have been recorded.

Temminck's stint *Calidris temminckii*. Normally three to six late May to early June, and two to four in autumn. Ten 15th May, 1980.

White-rumped sandpiper *Calidris fuscicollis*. Two 21st to 24th August, 1980, 11th September, 1980. One 31st July to 2nd August, 1981, 28th to 29th August, 1981, 15th May, 1986.

Pectoral sandpiper *Calidris melanotos*. One or two recorded most years in August–September. One 16th to 27th June and three 29th August, 1985.

Sharp-tailed sandpiper *Calidris acuminata*. One 27th to 28th August, 1979.

Dunlin *Calidris alpina*. From ten to thirty in spring, a few in summer, and up to 150 in autumn; scarce in winter.

Curlew sandpiper *Calidris ferruginea*. A few on spring passage, usually up to twenty in autumn. Forty-two on 14th August, 1982, sixty-six on 13th September, 1985.

Semipalmated sandpiper *Calidris pusilla*. One 4th June, 1977.

Sanderling *Calidris alba*. One to four recorded annually in spring and autumn.

Buff-breasted sandpiper *Trynites subruficollis*. One 9th August, 1975, 12th September to 1st October, 1979, 4th September, 1982.

Broad-billed sandpiper *Limicola falcinellus*. Recorded in late May on six occasions since 1975, one between late August and mid-September in several years.

Ruff *Philomachus pugnax*. Breeding species up to 1931. Present at all seasons, up to forty in winter. In spring up to 150 have occurred.

Avocet *Recurvirostra avosetta*. One pair bred 1949, and 1982 to 1987, but not successfully in 1986 and 1987; occurs on passage spring and autumn.

Black-winged stilt *Himantopus himantopus*. One 27th May, 1915, three 2nd August, 1922, two 24th May, 1929, one 17th June, 1968, 19th to 29th May, 1980.

Grey phalarope *Phalaropus fulicarius*. One 31st October, 1938, 29th May, 1975, 24th May, 1987.

Red-necked phalarope *Phalaropus lobatus*. Individuals recorded most years May to September; two 13th September, 1985.

Wilson's phalarope *Phalaropus tricolor*. One 17th to 25th June, 1971.

Stone curlew *Burhinus oedicnemus*. One pair nested close to the reserve 1943 and 1944.

Cream-coloured courser *Cursorius cursor*. One 17th to 18th June, 1913.

Arctic skua *Stercorarius parasiticus*. One 2nd August, 1975, 1st September, 1984, 24th July, 1985, 3rd August, 1986.

Pomarine skua *Stercorarius pomarinus*. One 21st September, 1914, 19th September, 1922, 22nd September, 1932.

Great black-backed gull *Larus marinus*. Present all year, in winter up to 300 may roost; a few immatures in summer.

Lesser black-backed gull *Larus fuscus*. One pair nested 1980; up to 400 spring to summer, mostly immatures. Adults of Scandinavian form *L. f. fuscus* often present in summer.

Herring gull *Larus argentatus*. Recorded in every month in small numbers. Adults of Scandinavian form *L. a. omissus* occur in summer.

Common gull *Larus canus*. Present all year; several hundred roost in winter, few in summer.

Glaucous gull *Larus hyperboreus*. Seven records up to 1944, none since.

Iceland gull *Larus glaucoides*. Singles recorded almost annually up to 1928, none since.

Mediterranean gull *Larus melanocephalus*. One 10th October, 1939, 17th June and 2nd September, 1979.

Bonaparte's gull *Larus philadelphia*. One 20th May, 1913, 6th May, 1927.

Little gull *Larus minutus*. One pair nested 1978, but eggs taken; occurs annually between late April and September, maximum twelve.

Black-headed gull *Larus ridibundus*. Resident, about fifty pairs breed but are controlled; huge winter roost on main broad.

Sabine's gull *Larus sabini*. One 16th July, 1912, 16th December, 1921, 19th September, 1935.

Kittiwake *Rissa tridactyla*. Nine records up to 1935; one 22nd January, 1976.

Black tern *Chlidonias niger*. Regular on passage spring and autumn, usually in small numbers, but about 500 on 14th May, 1980; one 22nd October, 1987.

White-winged black tern *Chlidonias leucopterus*. Formerly an irregular passage migrant; one 9th June, 1980, 10th May, 1987.

Whiskered tern *Chlidonias hybrida*. Eight records up to 1944, none since.

Gull-billed tern *Gelochelidon nelotica*. Six records up to 1944, none since.

Caspian tern *Hydroprogne caspia*. Five records up to 1944; two 17th to 26th June, 1959, one 10th September to 2nd October, 1959, one, sometimes two, 31st July to 12th August, 1973, one 7th May, 1983, 6th August, 1985, 23rd May to 5th July, 1987.

Aleutian tern *Sterna aleutica*. One 22nd to 24th June, 1986.

Common tern *Sterna hirundo*. Present from mid-April to September; has bred since 1953, up to sixteen pairs.

Arctic tern *Sterna paradisaea*. Recorded annually on passage in spring, and occasionally in autumn.

Roseate tern *Sterna dougallii*. One 6th May, 1936, two 13th May, 1976, one 27th May and 28th July, 1983, 24th to 29th May, 1985, 14th to 15th August, 1985.

Little tern *Sterna albifrons*. Present from late April to early September; between 1976 and 1979 up to forty-one pairs bred, but had declined to three pairs in 1986.

Sandwich tern *Sterna sandvicensis*. A few occur on passage spring and autumn.

Little auk *Alle alle*. Nine records up to 1944, none since.

Guillemot *Uria aalge*. One for several days in January, 1976.

Puffin *Fratercula artica*. One dead on broad 13th November, 1912.

Stock dove *Columba oenas*. A few pairs breed; winter flocks of about thirty.

Woodpigeon *Columba palumbus*. Common resident; large winter flocks.

Turtle dove *Streptopelia turtur*. Common summer visitor, up to sixteen breeding pairs.

Collared dove *Streptopelia decaocto*. Resident, a few pairs breed.

Cuckoo *Cuculus canorus*. Regular summer visitor, numerous in some years, breeds.

Great spotted cuckoo *Clamator glandarius*. One 29th July, 1941.

Barn owl *Tyto alba alba*. Resident, up to three pairs have bred in recent years; eleven pairs bred in Hickling parish in 1915.

Tawny owl *Strix aluco*. First recorded in 1924, first bred in 1937; now numerous resident and breeds; a pair nested on ground in 1943.

Long-eared owl *Asio otus*. Breeding species up to 1968, maximum five pairs; one 5th August, 1979, 8th September, 1981.

Short-eared owl *Asio flammeus*. Former breeding species, but now a rather scarce winter visitor; occasionally one in spring.

Nightjar *Caprimulgus europaeus*. Four records up to 1944; one 25th May, 1973, 28th May, 1976.

Swift *Apus apus*. Non-breeding summer visitor from late April to early September; often many hundreds over broad during summer.

Hoopoe *Upupa epops*. One 12th to 19th September, 1931, 17th May, 1939, 29th–30th April, 1950, 7th May, 1986.

Green woodpecker *Picus viridis*. Rare, no records prior to 9th August, 1977, when one present; one 16th March, 1978, 25th October, 1981, 8th to 17th August, 1986.

Great spotted woodpecker *Dendrocopos major*. Resident, up to four breeding pairs.

Lesser spotted woodpecker *Dendrocopos minor*. Resident, up to three breeding pairs; scarce in winter.

Wryneck *Jynx torquilla*. One or two occur annually in autumn, less regular in spring.

Woodlark *Lullula arborea*. One 18th September, 1976, 22nd September, 1978, 6th September, 1985.

Skylark *Alauda arvensis*. Common resident, breeding mainly confined to grazing marshes; large immigrations occur between October and December.

Shorelark *Eremophila alpestris*. Seven 29th November, 1922, one 18th to 20th November, 1976, 19th January, 1981; remarkable to record this away from the coast.

Swallow *Hirundo rustica*. Normally up to seven breeding pairs, but only two in 1987; thousands roost in reedbeds in autumn.

House martin *Delichon urbica*. A few pairs breed; many feed over broad in summer during rough weather.

Sand martin *Riparia riparia*. Does not breed; feeds over Broad, where often large congregations in late summer.

Golden oriole *Oriolus oriolus*. Irregular spring migrant; in 1983 single birds on five dates between 8th May and 5th June.

Carrion crow *Corvus corone corone*. Regular winter visitor up to 1944, when often fifty to a hundred recorded; now less regular, usually two to six.

Hooded crow *Corvus corone cornix*. Was a numerous winter visitor up to 1944; in 1978 and 1982 up to eight present, but usually only one or two.

Right: *A heron's pellet containing feathers and quills of a starling. The pellet is four and a half inches long.*
S. Linsell

Below: *A heron on its nest in Sounds Plantation.*   Dr K. J. Carlson

Rook *Corvus frugilegus.* Non-resident; often seen on or over the reserve; immigrants observed in late autumn.

Jackdaw *Corvus monedula.* Non-resident; a few pairs breed close to the reserve: immigrants observed in late autumn.

Magpie *Pica pica.* First recorded 22nd January, 1922; uncommon resident, one or two pairs occasionally breed; numerous in winter.

Nutcracker *Nucifraga caryocatactes.* One 15th July, 1924, 27th August, 1968.

Jay *Garrulus glandarius.* Resident, about twelve pairs breed; in October and November immigrants observed.

Great tit *Parus major.* Resident and common breeding species.

Blue tit *Parus cueruleus.* Resident and common breeding species; in winter small flocks occur in reedbeds.

Coal tit *Parus ater.* Non-resident; a few observed in woodlands in autumn and winter.

Marsh tit *Parus palustris.* A very scarce resident; a pair or two may breed.

Willow tit *Parus montanus montanus.* Numerous resident; up to ten breeding pairs.

Long-tailed tit *Aegithalos caudatus.* A fairly numerous resident and breeding species.

Penduline tit *Remiz pendulinus.* A male 4th to 9th April, 1987.

Nuthatch *Sitta europaea.* Two 19th August, 1986.

Treecreeper *Certhia familiaris.* Resident and breeds in the woods.

Wren *Troglodytes troglodytes.* Resident; but less widespread now due to severe winters in nineteen-eighties; frequents reedbeds in winter.

Bearded tit *Panurus biarmicus.* Resident; but has declined due to severe winters in nineteen-eighties; about 110 breeding pairs up to 1982, then declined to twenty-three pairs in 1987.

Mistle thrush *Turdus viseivorus.* Uncommon resident; one or two pairs breed.

Fieldfare *Turdus pilaris.* Winter visitor; but has been recorded in every month except July; often large flocks in autumn.

Song thrush *Turdus philomelos.* Resident and fairly numerous breeding species; many immigrants in autumn.

Redwing *Turdus iliacus.* Mainly an abundant autumn visitor, very few in winter; occasionally a return passage in late March.

Ring ouzel *Turdus torquatus.* Irregular on spring migration; a few occur annually late September to early November.

Blackbird *Turdus merula.* Resident and common breeding species; many immigrants in autumn.

Wheateater *Oenanthe oenanthe.* A pair nested in 1930; a few occur on passage spring and autumn; birds of Greenland race *Oe. oe. leucorrhoa* seen in May and September.

Stonechat *Saxicola torquata.* A pair nested 1932, 1941, and 1985; one or two regularly in winter up to 1979, when reed cutting was mechanised, none since then.

Whinchat *Saxicola rubetra.* Scarce on spring migration; a few occur September to early October, twelve on 21st September, 1981.

Redstart *Phoenicurus phoenicurus.* Rare on spring passage; a few observed annually September to early October.

148

Black redstart *Phoenicurus ochruros.* One 14th April, 1975, 18th April, 1982, 7th May, 1983, 16th April, 1985.

Nightingale *Luscinia megarhynchos.* One pair bred 1939 and 1984; rare on spring migration.

Bluethroat *Cyanosylvia svecica.* One 26th April, 1913, 14th May, 1915, 24th September, 1922, 2nd October, 1943; none since.

Robin *Erithacus rubecula.* Resident and common breeding species.

Cetti's warbler *Cettia cetti.* First recorded autumn 1977; one pair may have bred 1982–83; up to four pairs bred 1984–86; none 1987.

Grasshopper warbler *Locustella naevia.* Summer visitor, normally up to sixteen breeding pairs.

Savi's warbler *Locustella luscinioides.* First recorded 1974, then increased to eight singing males by 1982, now declined to one to three pairs breeding successfully.

Reed warbler *Acrocephalus scirpaceus.* Present from late April to mid-October, common breeding species.

Sedge warbler *Acrocephalus schoenobaenus.* Present from mid-April until mid-September, common breeding species.

Aquatic warbler *Acrocephalus paludicola.* One 6th September, 1978, 8th to 17th August, 1981.

Blackcap *Sylvia atricapilla.* Summer visitor, up to eight breeding pairs; numerous migrants September to mid-October.

Garden warbler *Sylvia borin.* One or two breeding pairs since 1978.

Whitethroat *Sylvia communis.* Up to eight breeding pairs until 1983, but had declined to five pairs in 1987.

Lesser whitethroat *Sylvia curruca curruca.* A few occur on passage in spring, two or three pairs breed in most years.

Willow warbler *Phyllosopus trochilus.* Common breeding species in all scrub and woodland areas.

Chiffchaff *Phylloscopus collybita.* An uncommon breeding species, usually only two or three pairs; Scandinavian race *P. c. abietinus* occurs occasionally in October.

Wood warbler *Phylloscopus sibilatrix.* A pair nested in 1944; rare on spring migration.

Goldcrest *Regulus regulus.* Small numbers occur on passage in autumn, a few winter.

Firecrest *Regulus ignicapillus.* One 6th October, 1976, 13th October, 1979, 29th October, 1983.

Spotted flycatcher *Muscicapa striata.* Migrants pass through in spring and autumn; three or four pairs breed in suitable areas.

Pied flycatcher *Ficedula hypoleuca.* A few occur on autumn passage most years; a female 14th June, 1975.

Dunnock *Prunella modularis.* Resident and common breeding species.

Richard's pipit *Anthus novaeseelandiae.* One 6th October, 1915, 18th October, 1923, 16th October, 1982.

Meadow pipit *Anthus pratensis.* A fairly common resident, up to twelve breeding pairs; migrant flocks occur in autumn.

Tree pipit *Anthus trivialis.* One or two occur most years in September.

Water pipit *Anthus spinoletta spinoletta.* Regular winter visitor, arriving in October and departing in April, usually up to six, but fourteen on 30th

January, 1984. A few Rock pipits *A. s. petrosus*, etc, late autumn.

Pied wagtail *Motacilla alba yarrelli*. Resident, about four breeding pairs; up to 100 roost in winter. Numerous white wagtails *M. a. alba* occur late March to early May.

Grey wagtail *Motacilla cinerea*. Very scarce migrant; four records in July or August, 1970 to 1980; one 4th April, 1984, two 27th September, 1986.

Yellow wagtail *Motacilla flava flavissima*. Formerly a common summer visitor, now only two or three pairs breed. Blue-headed race *M. f. flava* occurs regularly late April and May. Grey-headed race *M. f. thunbergi* often recorded late May to early June. One *M. f. feldegg* 8th May, 1986.

Waxwing *Bombycilla garrulus*. One 10th November, 1981.

Great grey shrike *Lanius excubitor*. One or two in most winters between November and early April.

Lesser grey shrike *Lanius minor*. One 21st September, 1914, an adult 28th October, 1983, for several days.

Red-backed shrike *Lanius collurio*. Nested up to 1943, now very irregular late August and September; one 17th October, 1977.

Starling *Sturnus vulgaris*. Resident, common breeding species; vast flocks roost in reedbeds between October and December.

Rose-coloured starling *Sturnus roseus*. One 12th June, 1983.

Hawfinch *Coccothraustes coccothraustes*. Four records up to 1944; one 6th May, 1978.

Greenfinch *Carduelis chloris*. Resident, a few pairs breed.

Goldfinch *Carduelis carduelis*. Scarce resident, one or two pairs breed; few in winter.

Siskin *Carduelis spinus*. Winter visitor only, in variable numbers.

Linnet *Acanthis cannabina*. Resident, a few pairs breed.

Twite *Acanthis flavirostris*. Irregular winter visitor.

Lesser redpoll *Acanthis flammea cabaret*. Resident, several pairs breed; up to 200 in winter, when one or more mealy redpools *A. f. flammea* occur.

Bullfinch *Pyrrhula pyrrhula*. Common resident and breeding species.

Crossbill *Loxia curvirostra*. Six on 25th March, 1979.

Chaffinch *Fringilla coelebs*. Fairly numerous resident, breeds; many immigrants occur in October and November.

Brambling *Fringilla montifringilla*. Small numbers on passage in autumn; occasionally a few winter.

Corn bunting *Emberiza calandra*. Eight on 18th February, 1976.

Yellowhammer *Emberiza citrinella*. Common resident and breeding species.

Cirl bunting *Emberiza cirlus*. Two on 13th April, 1936.

Ortolan bunting *Emberiza hortulana*. Two 20th September, 1922, one 9th September, 1985.

Rustic bunting *Emberiza rustica*. One 28th April, 1934.

Reed bunting *Emberiza schoeniclus*. Resident and common breeding species; few remain to winter.

Lapland bunting *Calcarius lapponicus*. One 14th November, 1982, and one 18th to 19th February, 1986.

Snow bunting *Plectrophenax nivalis*. Fourteen 27th November, 1977, twenty-four 15th February, 1978, two 2nd January, 1986.

House sparrow *Passer domesticus*. Common resident.

Tree sparrow *Passer montanus*. Resident, but not a common breeding species; often large flocks in winter.

(Records up to 1944 taken from Jim Vincent's diaries)

Some early records

Little crake *Porzana parva*. One shot 25th October, 1880.
Whiskered tern *Chlidonias hybrida*. One shot 17th June, 1847.
Pallas's sandgrouse *Syrrhaptes paradoxus*. Flock of twenty in June, 1906.
White's thrush *Turdus dauma*. One shot 10th October, 1871.
Cirl bunting *Emberiza cirlus*. Two shot October, 1875.

Recent 'escapes'

The following birds escaped from captivity were recorded at Hickling between 1975 and 1987:

Black swan *Cygnus atratus*.
Bar-headed goose *Anser indicus*.
Bahama pintail *Anas bahamensis*.
Rosybill *Netta peposaca*.
Mandarin *Aix galericulata*.
Carolina *Aix sponsa*.
Chilean flamingo *Phoenicopterus chilensis*.

Notes from the Vincent diaries, 1911–1944

Osprey: Recorded annually, one 10th January, 1944.
Hooded Crow: Common in winter, often up to 100, but 150 on 2nd April, 1930.
Snipe: Several hundred often recorded in autumn and winter, and twenty to forty jack snipe in most winters.
Barn owl: Nested annually, with ten pairs in Hickling parish in 1915.
First "oiled" gulls observed in 1922.
Bittern: Cannibalism first noted in 1927.
Montagu's harrier: First European photograph of bird on the nest 28th June, 1929. Best breeding year was 1921, when six pairs raised sixteen young.
Common scoter, scaup, smew, spoonbill, rough-legged buzzard, peregrine, little gull, water pipit and grey wagtail all recorded annually.
Eight reeve's eggs were brought from Holland and placed in four redshank's nests on 6th May, 1925. All hatched and later flew. Eight ruffs and two reeves were brought from the London Zoo by David Seth-Smith and released on 24th April, 1936. Mating observed, but nesting only suspected.

151

Entomological Notes

Lepidoptera

Contributed by Dr Tim Peet

The large area of reedbed and rough marsh that surrounds the open water of Hickling Broad provides a highly specialized habitat for a unique assembly of moths. Equally important are the areas of successional alder carr and the climax woodland areas of mature oak. The micro-climate of this part of Norfolk is influenced by its very flatness, the nearness of the sea, and the typical easterly winds. Winters tend to be very cold, often with snowfall; spring is late compared with more inland areas, and summers never as hot as in nearby Norwich.

Detailed records of the moths and butterflies of the reserve have been kept since 1958. Mercury-vapour light trap records have been centred on Whiteslea Lodge, but other areas have been regularly sampled including Whiteslea Wood, Catfield Dyke and Hickling Staithe. Twenty-four species of butterfly have been recorded and nearly 500 species of moths. The rarities among the moth population are perhaps less obvious than the swallowtail butterfly, which can rightly be regarded as Hickling's jewel, but the insect fauna as a whole emphasizes the importance of Hickling as a National Nature Reserve. The advent of moth trapping has enormously increased the number of species recorded, but the micro-lepidoptera are best found by sweeping, beating, and searching for larvae.

Hickling is probably the best viewing place for the swallowtail in the whole of Broadland. The British sub-species is not only different in appearance from the continental form but occupies a different habitat and is confined to one foodplant. Searching for larvae on the reserve has shown that while milk parsley is common, and in some areas abundant, eggs and larvae are found only in restricted areas. There has to be water fairly close to the foodplant, and eggs are never where milk parsley is overshadowed by trees and bushes. Cleared areas of overgrown marsh, which may have large stands of vigorous foodplant, do not usually have an accompanying excess of larvae. This habitat preference is a guide to the conservation of the butterfly and to sympathetic management of the habitat.

The population of swallowtails at Hickling appears stable, and allowing for annual fluctuations due to the weather there has been no marked change over the past twenty-five years. From early June to the end of July adults may be seen on the wing, surprisingly well camouflaged considering their size. For the photographer, ragged robin is the butterfly's first choice for nectar, and the swallowtail can most easily be approached when fluttering in front of flower heads. In hot summers a partial second brood of adults appears in August. Visitors in the tree hide in Whiteslea Wood may see the spiralling display flight, as yet not properly recorded in entomological literature.

The small oak woods around the broad and on the Skoyles Marsh nature trail contain a fine population of the purple hairstreak. This insect has only been noticed within the past five years, but because of its preference for the tops of trees may well have been overlooked. The butterflies are most active during the late afternoon, from about the last week of July until early September, and may be watched at eye level from the tree hide.

Among other striking butterflies is the peacock. The adults are particularly attracted to the flowers of hemp agrimony, and the larvae common on nettles, though frequently parasitized. In some seasons this butterfly is really abundant. Although Norfolk is not on a principal migration route, most years see examples of the painted lady. Resident, but at a low density, are the brimstone and the orange tip, both spring insects, and there is a small colony of the holly blue. In mid-summer bramble blossom is alive with the reserve's commonest butterfly, the gatekeeper, and there is a colony of the ringlet around the woods and on the Skoyles nature trail. There are two species of resident skipper, the large and the small. I have examined large numbers of the small skippers in order to discover whether the scarcer Essex skipper is present, but it does not seem to occur here.

Some comments follow on the reserve's more unusual moths, not always either large or obvious. The reed leopard (*Phragmataerea castaneae*) is common, the males "coming to light" from mid-June to early August. Larvae feed in the rootstocks of reed, and this moth is found only in Broadland. The marshland form of the five-spot burnet (*Zygaena trifolii* ssp. *decreta*) is now scarce throughout its range, but there is a small colony at Hickling; the larvae feed on the yellow marsh birdsfoot trefoil which climbs over the low vegetation at the edge of the sedge beds. A tiny moth with no English name, *Coleophora hydrolapathella*, was discovered at Hickling in 1976 and was then new to the British Isles. Its case-bearing larvae feed on the seeds of the great water dock, and are perfectly camouflaged within the dead heads of the foodplant. Among the Pyralid group of moths the rare *Eurrhypara perlucidalis* was discovered at Hickling in 1974, and apart from Wood Walton this was then the only British locality; it has since been discovered in one or two other spots. Two further local species are the deep red and white *Nascia cilialis* and the giant *Schoenobius gigantella*.

The bigger moths are more readily noticed by the casual observer. In April, the males of the day-flying emperor (*Saturnia pavonia*) are common, and the large green and black larvae are often noticed later in the year feeding on bramble. The oak eggar (*Lasiocampa quercus*) flies over the grazing marshes in July and is often mistaken for a butterfly. The drinker (*Philudoria potatoria*) is usually seen as a hairy caterpillar feeding on reed in April and May after hibernation; it is a favourite prey of cuckoos. The adult moths are common to light in August.

The Geometrid group contains only a few specialities. The most noticeable is a strong population of the rosy wave (*Scopula emutaria*), and two good pug moths: the valerian pug (*Eupethecia valerianata*) and the

153

dentate pug (*Anticollix sparsata*). Larvae of the latter may be found commonly on yellow loosestrife.

Eight species of hawk-moth have been recorded, of which the most unusual resident is the small elephant (*Deilephila porcellus*). Even the lime hawk (*Mimas tiliae*) turns up occasionally, wandering from further inland.

I have never found puss moth larvae (*Cerura vinula*), but the adult males "come to light" in May, and a single egg was found on a sallow leaf and bred through. Scarcer is the alder kitten (*Furcula bicuspis*), of which on average one is noted each year. Hedgerow field maple provides the foodplant for the maple prominent (*Ptilodontella cucullina*), also seen as an occasional visitor.

Hawthorn hedges and trees are often covered with the hairy larvae of the yellowtail (*Euproctis similis*), and the less common white satin (*Leucoma salicis*) is frequent to light. The Arctiid moths (tigers and footmen) have two really scarce local species among them. The dotted footman (*Pelosia muscerda*) is fairly frequently found at Hickling in late July; Broadland is its principal habitat in the British Isles. Even more local is the small dotted footman (*Pelosia obtusa*), confined solely to Hickling and Barton. A small and inconspicuous insect, it appears to be confined to sedge beds, and is apparently reluctant to fly to light. More often seen as a larva than as an adult is the water ermine (*Spilosoma urticae*), which is frequent on the reserve.

The large group of Noctuid moths are almost wholly nocturnal and are observed only if collected from a moth trap or by rearing larvae. The wainscot group is particularly well represented. The most local are the obscure wainscot (*Mythimna obsoleta*), which is scarce at Hickling, and the flame wainscot (*Senta flammae*), which is common. This latter species is associated with large reedbeds and is found only in the marshes of East Anglia, with a few small colonies along the south coast. The mere wainscot (*Photedes fluxa*), whose larva feeds on Calamagrostis, has been taken only twice. Fenns' wainscot (*Photedes brevilinea*) was first discovered at Ranworth over 100 years ago and is very common at Hickling; its only other locality outside Broadland is the Suffolk reedbeds around Walberswick. The cottongrass of the grazing marshes is the foodplant of Haworth's minor (*Celaena haworthii*), more common as a northern moorland species.

The reed-stem-boring wainscots are also well represented. The scarcer species include Webb's wainscot (*Archanara sparganii*), almost totally confined to coastal marshes, and the rarer rush wainscot (*Archanara algae*). The silky wainscot (*Chilodes maritimus*), which occurs throughout East Anglia, is common on the reserve and includes some very variable forms.

In recent years the common gold spot (*Plusia festucae*) has been subdivided into two species, and the marsh-loving Lempke's gold spot (*Plusia gracilis*) has been found to be common at Hickling, together with its near relative. A very local marshland moth, the dotted fanfoot (*Macrochilo cribrumalis*), is frequent at Hickling, but is virtually unknown outside East Anglia.

None of the species listed above are local because of limitation by a scarce foodplant, except possibly *C. hydrolapathella*. Several factors are responsible for this aggregation of unusual residents. The vegetation, the climate, and the very size of the reserve all contribute. Other parts of the reserve can compensate for local fluctuations in populations within tiny areas. The overall moth population resembles that to be found in northern and western Europe, as opposed to the warmer regions of France and the Mediterranean.

Many migrant species have been noted, but never in great numbers. Most represent a drift from northern Europe and Scandinavia rather than from further south. In 1976 there were many sightings all over Norfolk, although not on the Hickling reserve, of the Camberwell beauty, accompanied by the Clifden nonpareil (*Catocala fraxini*) and the goldenrod brindle (*Lithomoia solidaginis*). From further south have come such moths as the striped hawk (*Hyeles livorica*) and the convolvulus hawk (*Herse convolvuli*).

The closest source of migrants, albeit windblown, is the nearby coastal strip from Sea Palling to Winterton. Examples of the lyme-grass wainscot (*Photedes elymi*), the archer dart (*Agrotis vestigialis*) and the very local pygmy footman (*Eilema pygmaeola*) have all occurred annually.

Butterflies recorded up to 1987

Papilio machaon	Swallowtail
Pieris brassicae	Large white
Pieris rapae	Small white
Pieris napi	Green-veined white
Anthocharis cardamines	Orange tip
Gonepteryx rhamni	Brimstone
Limenitis camilla	White admiral*
Inachis io	Peacock
Vanessa atalanta	Red admiral
Vanessa cardui	Painted lady
Aglais urticae	Small tortoiseshell
Polygonia C-album	Comma*
Clossiana selene	Small pearl-bordered fritillary
Aphantopus hyperantus	Ringlet
Maniola jurtina	Meadow brown
Pyronia tithonus	Gatekeeper
Coenonympha pamphilus	Small heath
Lasiommata megera	Wall brown
Quercusia quercus	Purple hairsteak
Lycaena philaeas	Small copper
Celastrina argiolus	Holly blue
Polymmatus icarus	Common blue
Thymelicus sylvestris	Small skipper
Ochlodes venatus	Large skipper

* two records

Coleoptera

The Great Silver Water Beetle (*Hydrophilus piceus*), the largest of our British beetles, measuring almost two inches in length and one inch in breadth, is now believed to exist only in Broadland and the Somerset levels. While the larvae of this beetle are carnivorous, the adults are herbivorous. At Hickling it is now of almost annual occurrence and is occasionally taken at a mercury vapour light.

Odonata (dragonflies)

Contributed by Ivan Loades

1	*Aeshna cyanea* – The southern aeshna	C
2	*Aeshna grandis* – The brown aeshna	C
3	*Aeshna mixta* – The 'scarce' aeshna	C
4	*Brachytron pratense* – The hairy dragonfly	R
5	*Orthetrum cancellatums* – The black-tailed skimmer	S
6	*Libellula quadrimaculata* – The four-spotted libellula	C
7	*Sympetrum striolatum* – The common sympetrum	C/VC
8	*Lestes sponsa* – The emerald damselfly	C
9	*Pyrrhosoma nymphula* – The large red damselfly	S
10	*Ischnura elegans* – The blue-tailed damselfly	VC
11	*Enallagma cyathigerum* – The common blue damselfly	R
12	*Coenagrion puella* – The common coenagrion	C
13	*Coenagrion pulchellum* – The variable damselfly	C
14	*Aeshna isosceles* – The Norfolk aeshna	D
15	*Libellula fulva* – The scarce chaser	D
16	*Aeshna juncea* – The common hawker	VR/D

VC	=	Very common
C	=	Common
S	=	Scarce
R	=	Rare
VR	=	Very rare
D	=	Status doubtful

Notes to aid the identification of Hickling's dragonflies.

1. *Aeshna cyanea*

Common, late June to October. Territorial. Very large size makes it the biggest species seen at Hickling. Often inquisitive, making close encounters with humans—to within a few feet of observer. Flies often till late evening on warm summer evenings. Likes neighbouring wooded areas near water and under trees. Males have blue on last two segments, females green.

2. *Aeshna grandis*

Common, July to end September. Very territorial. Large, chocolate-bodied, with segments divided by thin lemon-yellow bars. Male has blue spots on two—three segments. Both sexes have honey-coloured clouded wings—only British species without clear wings. Very wary toward human approaches. Sexes similar. Lays eggs singly under muddy banks of ponds and sluggish streams.

3. *Aeshna mixta*

Common, July to October. Less territorial than *A. cyanea* and *A. grandis*. Smaller than *A. cyanea* and *A. grandis*. Males on wing appear bluer than browner females. Both sexes often fly high over trees when hawking insects. Very difficult to approach closely—great patience and care required. Once, as common name (scarce aeshna) suggests, rare, but now widespread and quite common. Often one of last species seen in the year, flying till first frosts.

4. *Brachytron pratense*

Rare at Hickling, as in most Norfolk haunts. Not significantly territorial. Several individuals may occupy same stretch of stream. Size of *A. mixta*. First dragonfly on the wing from mid-May to end of June. Close inspection reveals hairy thorax, more than any other British species. Wings a little dumpier than other Aeshnas. Males bluish in general appearance on the wing, females brown yellow. Usually fly nearer sluggish streams and dykes on edge of carrs, beating back and forth.

5. *Orthetrum cancellatum*

Scarce, early June to August. Males powder blue with black tail-end (last two segments) (*O. coerulescens* males all blue bodies—*not* a Hickling species) and black thorax and prothorax. Females honey brown all over with striking black pairs of longitudinal segment marks each side of a thin continuous mid line down length of body. Young males often seen looking like female until blue colour matures. Male likes sunning itself on bare mud patches at edge of water. Females prefer some vegetation cover.

6. *Libellula quadrimaculata*

Common, end of May to mid August, males gregarious at times. As common name suggests, both sexes, which are generally dark, dull brown in general appearance, have two spots (black) on each forward wing—one at tip (the pterastigma) and another half way along. A dark diffused patch at base of wings. Ceaseless flyers up and down reed-bordered dykes, occasionally resting on an overhanging weed or stem. Frequently leaves the dyke edge to make quick darting sorties inland in a short circle before returning to its regular beat along the dyke. Very wary.

7. *Sympetrum striolatum*

Common to very common, June to October. Colonial. Probably Britain's commonest "true" dragonfly. Males bright red bodied, females honey coloured, and young males often similar to females with little of the adult red showing. Frequently settles to bask on bare/sandy areas or on tree stumps etc. Often many individuals seen in close proximity. Fairly approachable. Pairs fly in tandem during mating and often while female is egg-laying at the surface of a pond. As with *A. mixta*, flies till late October.

8. *Lestes sponsa*

Common, mid June to end September. Gregarious (often great densities). Both sexes a metallic green. Males with blue on first two and last two segments, also body where wings join it. Females brownish tail end and honey brown where wings meet body. NB: very careful study of anal appendages is needed to differentiate *L. sponsa* from the similar *L. dryas* (now very, very rare and not known from Hickling area). Loves resting in reedy bankside vegetation by small streams and well matured dykes. Easy to approach, not given to flying much.

9. *Pyrrhosoma nymphula*

Scarce to common, mid May to August. Small colonies. Both sexes have bright crimson eyes with similarly red bodies with black bars dividing body segments. In some lights the artehumeral stripes on the thorax appear decidedly bronze-coloured, otherwise red or orange, according to age. One of the first damsels to appear in the spring near water, often brackish. Easily approached to observe at close quarters.

10. *Ischnura elegans*

Very common, early June to end of August. Forms large communities. Another very common and widespread species, nearly always present with other species. Both sexes black bodied with blue band on "tail" (ninth segment). Occupies similar sites and regularly present with *L. sponsa* and *P. nymphula*. Flies low among dyke vegetation, spending most of the day at rest on stems until disturbed.

11. *Enallagma cyathigerum*

Scarce to rare, mid-May to late August. One of three "blue damsels" to be seen at Hickling. Body of males powder blue with several black areas along body. Females dark coloured. Certain identification only by studying markings on second segment. This species marking may be described as a "ball and chain". Likes open areas of water. Fairly approachable but difficult to get close to see second-segment marks.

12. *Coenagrion puella* — Common, mid-May to mid-August. Tolerant in behaviour towards other species. Similar to *E. cyathigerum*, but second segment marking is like a wine glass without the stem. Females black with small blue tail segment. Often in company with *C. pulchellum* (next species described here), so careful study of the second segment is required. Found by dykes and fringe of the broad.

13. *Coenagrion pulchellum* — Scarce to common, mid-May to August. Behaviour similar to *C. puella*. Colouring very similar to *C. puella*, but mark on second segment is a "Mercury" sign (females). In the female the mark is a complete wine glass shape. Often found in water meadows, as with *C. puella*. Both these species are difficult to approach closely for identification of segment marks.

14. *Aeshna isosceles*
15. *Libellula fulva*
16. *Aeshna juncea* — These three species may be recorded from Hickling area, but not seen by I. Loades [author]. For identification and behaviour suggest reference to book recommended below for identification of all British species.

Recommended Field Guide — *The Dragonflies of Great Britain and Ireland.* C. O. Hammond. Curwen. 1st Edition 1977. Now available in 2nd Edition also.

Appendix three

Botanical Notes

Contributed by Dr James Cadbury

Until the mid-nineteen-sixties one of the outstanding features of the shallow calcareous and slightly brackish waters of Hickling Broad and the adjoining Whiteslea and Heigham Sounds was the prolific growth of aquatic plants, notably stoneworts (*Charaphytes*), of which nine species were recorded. The area was also rich in pondweeds. The most plentiful of these was the fennel-leaved pondweed with large orbicular fruits, much favoured by such wildfowl as pochard. Also frequent was the holly-leaved naiad, a national rarity confined in Britain to Hickling and a few neighbouring broads. It still occurs on Hickling in a few relatively undisturbed areas. Many sheltered backwaters and dykes were choked with free-floating plants such as bladderwort, frog-bit, and water soldier with its rosettes of spiky leaves.

Where once you could look down on to a forest of aquatic plants in enticingly clear water during the summer months, there is now a "soupy" opaqueness. A proliferation of minute planktonic algae and a suspension of fine silt and clay particles accounts for the turbidity of the water, which reduces light penetration, inhibiting photosynthesis by submerged aquatic plants. Moreover, the firm clay floor of the broad in most places lies buried beneath a deep and soft layer of sediment. It is believed that seedlings may find it difficult to become established in this sediment when it is disturbed by the passage of motor craft. Frog-bit and water soldier are among the species vulnerable to damage by thrashing boat propellers, and it is possibly for this reason that they have disappeared from Catfield Dyke at the west end of the broad. Marestail and the fennel-like pondweed are two of the few aquatic macrophytes which have not become markedly scarcer in Hickling Broad in recent years. They are desirable plants to have on a wildfowl refuge because the foliage and seeds are much favoured by wildfowl.

A feature that is obvious to anyone visiting Hickling Broad is the extensive swamp dominated by reed. Closer inspection, however, will reveal a succession of plant communities extending landward from the open water. On the outer margin of the swamp, shielding the reedbed, there are often floating rafts ("hovers") of lesser reedmace. Reed flourishes best in about a metre of water, but it soon builds up a mat of rhizomes and roots above the spongy peat. In the waterlogged transitional zone between the reedswamp and drier fen grows an assemblage of such plants as the broad-leaved great water dock, the poisonous cowbane, purple loosestrife, hemp agrimony and the dainty marsh fern.

Where water circulation is restricted, fen sedge or saw sedge tends to succeed reed as the dominant plant. At Hickling, saw sedge, with its razor-sharp leaf edges and triangular stems, is cut for roof ridge thatching. In late July the white flower heads of milk parsley, the purple-red blooms of hemp agrimony, the brilliant yellow loosestrife and the attractive meadowsweet are features of fen areas. Milk parsley not only has a restricted distribution in Britain, but is the food plant of the caterpillars of the swallowtail butterfly. In the vicinity of Catfield Dyke the fen is dominated by fen rush, black bog rush and purple moor-grass. Purple small-reed and the local marsh pea are also frequent in these areas, which may have been formerly mown for hay. In the absence of mowing, alder and sallow invade the drier parts of the fen to form carr. The narrow buckler fern is one of the characteristic ferns that grow in the spongy peat at the base of the bushes. In a few places at Hickling it is associated with the rare crested buckler.

Where the sward is kept artificially short by grazing and mowing, plants which cannot compete with taller vegetation thrive. Thus on the grazing marshes there is a good show of meadow thistle and a profusion of both marsh and spotted orchids in June. The procumbent sea milkwort is abundant beside the road to Whiteslea Lodge, as well as on the margins of some of the wader pools. It is normally associated with saltmarshes, as is scurvy-grass, which when in flower in May forms a splash of white in several areas. The presence of such plants inland at Hickling is an indication of the saline water table which underlies the whole area and which makes the water of the broad and the adjoining marsh ditches brackish. Those visiting the tree tower in Whiteslea Wood in summer may notice the delicate climbing corydalis with creamy flowers growing on peaty ground at the edge of the wood. It is also common beside pathways on the nature trails.

Many people visiting the area spend most of their time on a boat, from which they can see two handsome plants. The first is the fen or marsh sowthistle, which since it grows to a height of three metres overtops the reeds. It is a very local plant in Britain, but is spreading along the banks of the River Thurne and has now reached Hickling Broad. It is also plentiful along Meadow Dyke between Heigham Sounds and Horsey Mere. Those travelling by boat to Horsey, or between Martham and Somerton, may notice stands of marsh mallow on the bank. This plant of coastal marshes has pubescent grey-green leaves and in August produces rose-pink flowers.

Plants of the Fens and Marshes

Dryopteris cristata	Crested fern
Dryopteris dilatata	Broad buckler-fern
Osmunda regalis	Royal fern
Ranunculus acris	Meadow buttercup
Corydalis claviculata	Climbing corydalis
Cardamine pratensis	Cuckoo flower
Viola palustris	Bog violet
Polygala serpyllifolia	Heath milkwort
Lychnis flos-cuculi	Ragged robin

Silene alba	White campion
Silene dioica	Red campion
Stellaria palustris	Marsh stitchwort
Geranium versicolor	Streaked cranesbill
Lathyrus palustris	Marsh pea
Lotus uliginosus	Birdsfoot trefoil
Vicia sepium	Bush vetch
Eupatorium cannabinum	Hemp agrimony
Filipendula ulmaria	Meadowsweet
Potentilla erecta	Common tormentil
Potentilla anserina	Silverweed
Rosa canina	Dog rose
Lythrum salicaria	Purple loosestrife
Geum rivale	Water avens
Chamaenerion angustifolium	Rosebay willowherb
Epilobium adenocaulon	Great willowherb
Angelica sylvestris	Wild angelica
Peucedanum palustre	Milk parsley
Torilis japonica	Upright hedge parsley
Rumex hydrolapathum	Great water dock
Anagallis arvensis	Scarlet pimpernel
Centaurium erythraea	Common centaury
Symphytum officinale	Common comfrey
Solanum dulcamara	Woody nightshade
Solanum nigrum	Black nightshade
Digitalis purpurea	Foxglove
Pedicularis sylvatica	Lousewort
Mentha aquatica	Water mint
Prunella vulgaris	Selfheal
Scutellaria galericulata	Skullcap
Plantago major	Great plantain
Galium palustre	Marsh bedstraw
Lonicera periclymenum	Honeysuckle
Valeriana officinalis	Valerian
Cirsium arvense	Creeping thistle
Cirsium dissectum	Meadow thistle
Cirsium palustre	Marsh thistle
Hypochaeris radicata	Catsear
Senecio jacobaea	Common ragwort
Senecio sylvaticus	Wood groundsel
Tussilago farfara	Coltsfoot
Eriophorum angustifolium	Common cotton-grass
Juncus conglomeratus	Compact rush
Juncus effusus	Soft rush
Juncus inflexus	Hard rush
Iris pseudacorus	Yellow iris
Dactylorchis fuchsii	Spotted orchid
Carex otrubae	False fox-sedge
Carex pendula	Pendulous sedge
Carex riparia	Greater pond-sedge

Cladium mariscus	Fen or saw sedge
Ulex europaeus	Common gorse
Sarothamnus scoparius	Broom
Sorbus aucuparia	Rowan
Crataegus monogyna	Common hawthorn
Sambucus nigra	Elder
Fraxinus excelsior	Ash
Betula pendula	Silver birch
Alnus glutinosa	Alder
Frangula alnus	Alder buckthorn
Quercus robur	Oak
Salix alba	White willow
Salix cinerea	Sallow
Populus tremula	Aspen

Most of the above plants may be seen on the nature trails. Many other species occur on the reserve.

Plants of the Waterways and Dykes

Hippuris vulgaris	Marestail
Myriophyllum spicatum	Spiked water milfoil
Ceratophyllum demersum	Hornwort
Potamogeton pectinatus	Fennel-like pondweed
Najas marina	Holly-leaved naiad
Elodes canadensis	Canadian pondweed
Utricularia vulgaris	Bladderwort
Potamogeton lucens	Shining pondweed
Polygonum persicaria	Common persicaria
Alisma plantago-aquatica	Water plantain
Baldellia ranunculoides	Lesser water plantain
Hottonia palustris	Water violet
Jincus articulatus	Jointed rush
Mentha aquatica	Water mint
Potamogeton freisii	Flat-stalked pondweed
Potamogeton natans	Floating pondweed
Potamogeton pusillus	Small pondweed
Sparganium erectum	Branched bur-reed
Phragmites communis	Common reed
Typha angustifolia	Lesser reed-mace
Callitriche stagnalis	Starwort
Lemna trisulca	Ivy duckweed
Sonchus palustris	Fen or giant sowthistle

Appendix four

Notes on Some Mammals

Although the majority of visitors come to Hickling to enjoy its bird life, butterflies, dragonflies and flora they may also observe, albeit briefly, some of the mammals which inhabit the marshes and woods.

Red deer *Cervus elephas*. Certainly the arrival of red deer in this wetland habitat in 1981 caused quite a stir. Early that year an adult pair was seen, and in mid-year they were observed with two young. In the autumn another hind joined them and all remained until the end of the year. In 1982 the five were seen together on 25th April and stayed until the end of the year, but no young were born. The five were joined by another five in September, 1983, and there were now two stags and eight hinds. During 1984 two herds of eight and ten were present within the parish, but only the eight were often seen on the reserve and a single young was born. In 1985 one herd kept to the north-east of the parish while the other of nine was regularly sighted throughout the year. On many occasions this herd was seen in the vicinity of the warden's house, and as in previous years the roaring of the stag was a feature of the rutting season. No young were seen that year. In 1986 two young were added to the reserve herd, while to the north farmers reported that the other herd numbered at least twelve, and damage was being caused to their crops. In 1987 it was believed the two herds totalled twenty-six, and local farmers felt strongly that their numbers must be culled because of the damage to crops, but no steps had been taken to do this up to October, 1987, when I left.

Fallow deer *Dama dama*. There are only two known sightings of single animals in the mid-seventies, when one was seen near the warden's house and another in the car park at Whiteslea Lodge.

Roe deer *Capreolus capreolus*. Singles observed from time to time since 1978, usually at the west end of the reserve.

Chinese water deer *Hydropotes inermis*. Have been fairly widespread in areas of fen and carr as well as reedbeds for many years. Very occasionally one or more have been seen from bird-hides.

Muntjac *Muntiacus reevesii*. Singles recorded on only four occasions between 1975 and 1987, and one of these was picked up dead.

Water vole *Arvicola amphibius*. A feature for a number of years was the presence of two melanistic forms in the vicinity of Whiteslea Lodge. These were last seen in 1983. Fairly common about the reserve.

Fox *Vulpes vulpes*. Fairly widespread over the reserve and outside it. In some years they cause considerable predation to nesting birds, particularly to waders, terns and gulls on the wader pools. When the waterways have been frozen over individuals have been seen walking on the broad beside the reed fringes. In some years visitors have reported seeing one or more from bird-hides. From time to time local farmers and the warden have carried out culls on the population.

Grey squirrel *Sciurus carolinensis*. Resident in variable numbers. Can prove a predator on small birds and their nests. In most years its numbers were kept under control, but in 1986 there was a notable increase in numbers in woodlands on both sides of the broad, and in the following winter and spring over two dozen were shot.

Stoat *Mustela erminea*. Another predator which has to be kept under control, otherwise nesting birds, especially on wader pools, can be decimated. May be seen dashing along a pathway on the nature trail or round the margins of a wader pool. Was twice observed swimming in Hickling Broad. Six were trapped in 1986.

Weasel *Mustela nivalis*. Less frequently seen than the stoat, usually in or near the garden of the warden's house.

Mink *Mustela vison*. Between 1975 and 1987 was occasionally reported by reserve staff and Hickling marshmen while reed harvesting. Only one summer sighting of a singleton near Deary's pool.

Coypu *Myocaster coypus*. Once abundant, but it is now believed to be extinct

A young coypu at the entrance to the burrow.
S. Linsell

following several years of intensive trapping by Coypu Control and some severe winters.

Hare *Lepus capensis*. Frequently observed between autumn and spring, when up to six or more may be seen on grazing marshes and adjoining arable fields as well as along the Whiteslea Lodge road.

Mole *Talpa europaea*. Resident and quite numerous, and not only in the warden's garden. Favours the flood-banks of the broad, which it burrows through, causing leaks. Sometimes observed swimming across wader pools and dykes.

Index

Illustrations in **bold type**

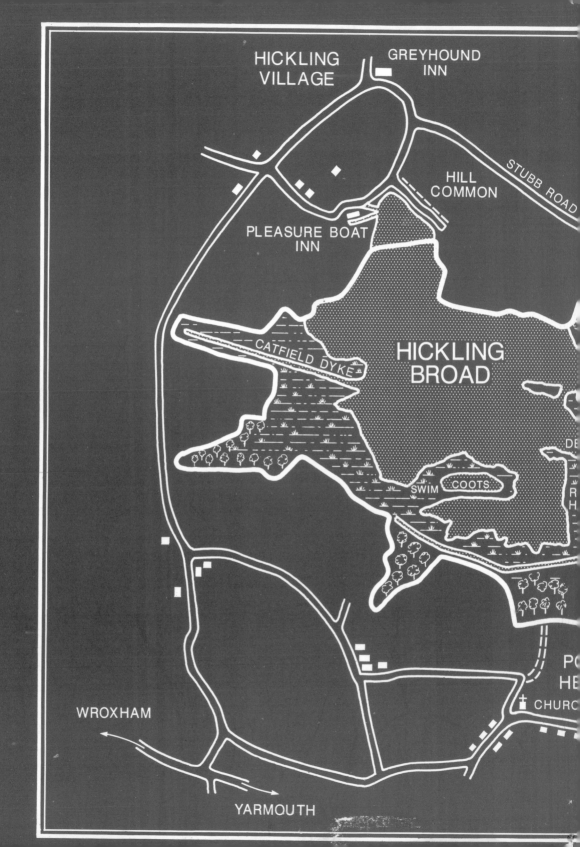